ISLAM:
Doctrines, Practices & Morals

by Mohammad Ali Shomali

Islam: Doctrines, Practices & Morals

Author: Mohammad Ali Shomali
First Edition: 2007
Quantity: 3000

ISBN: 978-1-904934-06-6

ALL RIGHTS RESERVED.

Published by

**Institute of Islamic Studies,
Islamic Centre of England**
140 Maida Vale
London W9 1QB, UK
Tel: 020 7604 5500
www.ic-el.com

In the Name of God the Beneficent the Merciful

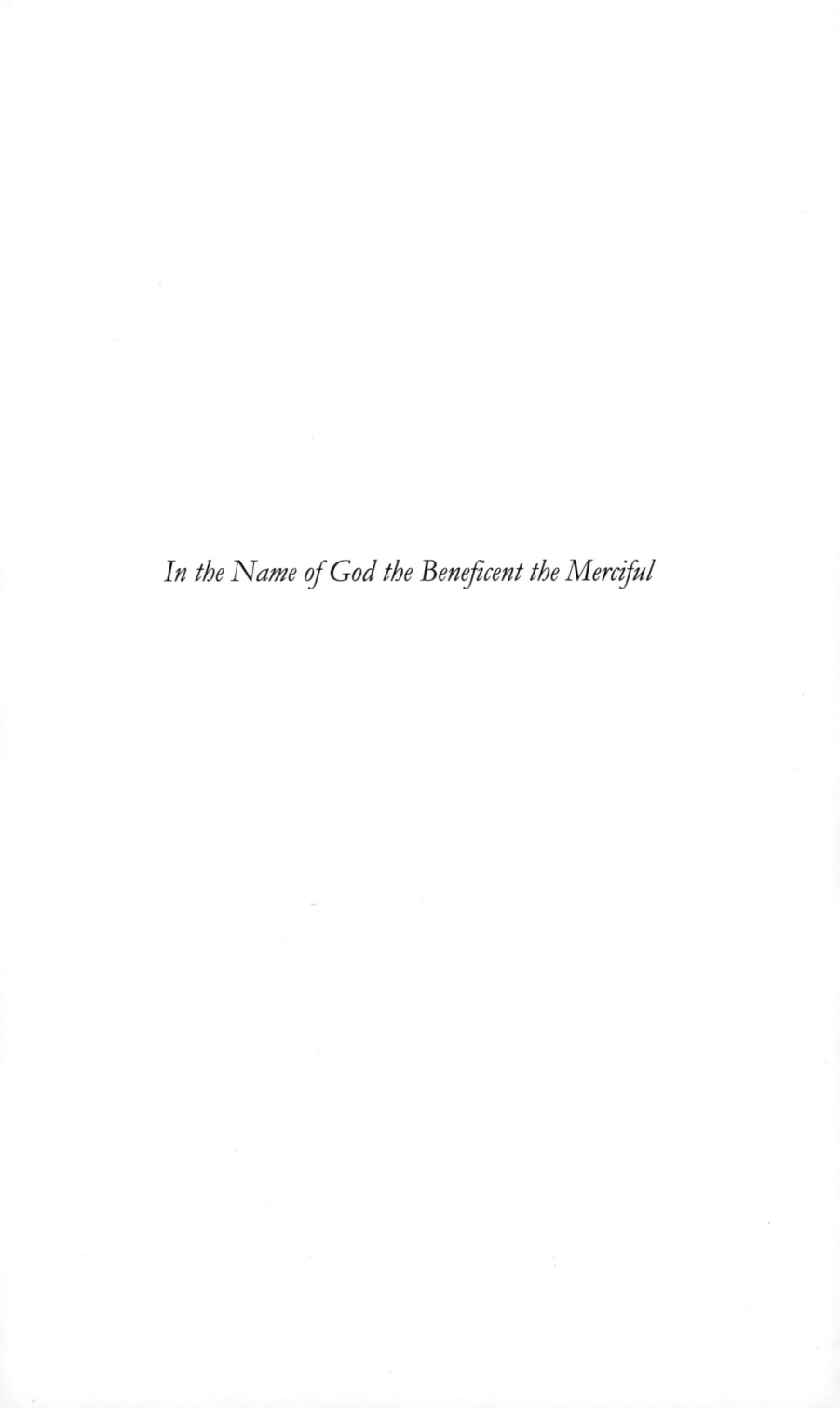

CONTENTS

CONTENTS 5

INTRODUCTION 7

CHAPTER 1 SOURCES OF ISLAMIC THOUGHT 13

THE GLORIOUS QUR'AN 13
THE SUNNAH 14
THE HOUSEHOLD OF THE PROPHET 17
   Who constitute the household of the Prophet? 21
REASON 23

CHAPTER 2 DOCTRINES 27

UNITY OF GOD 28
   Divine justice 29
PROPHETHOOD 30
   Imāmah 31
RESURRECTION 35
   Note 36

CHAPTER 3 PRACTICES 39

1. THE DAILY PRAYERS 39
2. FASTING 40
3. PILGRIMAGE TO MECCA 41
4. ALMSGIVING 43
5. STRUGGLE FOR THE SAKE OF GOD 45
6. ENJOINING GOOD AND FORBIDDING EVIL 48

CHAPTER 4 ISLAMIC MORALITY 49

MORAL SYSTEM OF ISLAM 52
   I Relationship with God 53
   II Relationship with one's self 54
   III Relationship with other people 61

IV Relationship with the environment 69
OUTCOMES OF LIVING A LIFE OF FAITH 71
SUPPLICATION 75

CHAPTER 5 THE MUSLIMS IN THE WORLD 77

HOLY CITIES 79
- *Mecca* 79
- *Medina* 79
- *Jerusalem* 81
- *Najaf* 82
- *Karbala* 82
- *Kadhimayn* 82
- *Samarra* 83
- *Mashhad* 83
- *Qum* 84

BIBLIOGRAPHY 87

INTRODUCTION

Islam is the second largest and the fastest growing religion in the world. Today Islam is the most discussed religion in the media, but at the same time, according to many, it is the most misunderstood religion as well. Certainly there are political reasons who contribute to this, but it is also partially because of the fact that interest in knowing more about Islam and Muslim affairs has grown so fast that qualified scholars could not cope with the high demand and as a result there remained some gap that sometimes unqualified people filled. The other problem is that despite all the great things that Muslims share sometimes so much attention is paid to the differences that outsiders may get confused about what really Islam is.

A careful study of all major Islamic schools shows that what they have in common is much more than what they differ about. All Muslims believe in the same God, the same Prophet and the same Qur'an. They all believe in the Day of Resurrection and divine rewards and punishments. They all say their daily prayers towards the same direction, that is, Mecca. They all fast the whole month of Ramadan. They all perform pilgrimage to Mecca (*hajj*) at the same time. They all believe in giving alms, enjoining good and forbidding evil. They all believe that they should make friends with the people of faith and good intention and keep away from enemies of God. They all adhere to the same virtues and values. According to the Qur'an, all believers are "brothers". Regardless of their colour, race, gender, and denomination, there are certain duties towards each other that brothers and sisters in faith must discharge.

Once Mu'alla b. Khunays asked Imam Sadiq about what one Muslim owes another. Imam replied: "There are seven duties incumbent upon him. Should he neglect but one of them, he is not a friend (or a servant) of God, and truly he has done nothing for the sake of God".

Then Imam mentioned the following:

a) Wish for your brother what you wish for yourself, and wish that what you do not desire for yourself should not befall your brother.

b) Do not make your brother angry, but seek to please him and obey his wishes.

c) Help him with your soul, your property, your tongue, your hands and your feet.

d) Be the eye that he sees with, his guide and his mirror.

e) Do not eat your fill when he is hungry, nor drink and clothe yourself when he is thirsty and naked.

f) If he has no servant, but you do, it is incumbent on you to send your servant to him to wash his clothes, cook his food and spread out his mattress.

g) Accept his promise and his invitation; visit him when he is sick, attend his funeral, and see to his needs before he asks you, hurrying to do them if you can. (Muzaffar, pp. 76 & 77).

Unfortunately, there have always been some short-sighted people among each group or sect who have tried to magnify the differences and have called for separation instead of unity and brotherhood. They hasten to find some excuses to call anyone who disagrees with them a *kāfir* (disbeliever) or a *mushrik* (polytheist) and any act that does not please them *bid'ah* (heresy). Of course, there are disbelievers and there are heretics, but one must be very cautious in applying these terms. Great Islamic leaders and scholars, whether they be Sunni or Shi'a, have never attached these labels to each other. In this way, they have represented in their fatwas, sayings and deeds the real spirit of Islam, this harmonious and universal message of peace, justice, unity and mercifulness.

Islam brought unity and solidarity for those who suffered a great deal from enmity and hostility (3:103). This act of unifying people is highly esteemed as a divine act (8:63). On the contrary, the action of people such as Pharaoh was to disunite people (28:4). The Qur'an warns believers that if they start disputing with each other they will weaken and they will, therefore, be defeated (8:46).

In fact, the call for unity is not limited to Muslims. The Qur'an invites all people of faith such as Christians and Jews to unify their efforts and concentrate on their common ground (3:64). Let us hope and pray that day by day this sense of unity and solidarity intensifies.

I should also note that the author is sincerely and wholeheartedly committed to unity of all believers and hopes that this work can serve as a modest step towards such unity. In fact, one of the best means of achieving this unity is to know each other and to overcome the historical prejudices that prevent objective understanding between each other. According to what Imam Ali has said, "People are enemies of what they do not know".

The present work aims to briefly address main issues related to Islam. The ideas presented here are based on common sources among the Muslims and unless otherwise mentioned, they represent Muslim faith in its most general form and are thought to be accepted by all. Though simply and clearly written, this is an outcome of twenty five years of involvement in Islamic studies, and based to some extent on some of my previous works and my experiences in giving talks to Muslims and non-Muslims in the west.

The first chapter studies the sources of Islamic thought, i.e. the Qur'an, the Sunnah and reason. Discussing the status of the Qur'an, the chapter goes on to establish that Muslims believe that the Qur'an which is present today is an embodiment of divine revelation to the Prophet Muhammad. The chapter continues by explaining the second most important source, i.e. the Sunnah, which includes the sayings and actions of the Prophet Muhammad. The Qur'an itself asks Muslims to take the Prophet as their role model, to refer to him to judge and settle their conflicts, and speaks of the Prophet as the one who recites, teaches and explains the Qur'an. In this chapter there is also a discussion about the household of the Prophet (*Ahlul Bayt*) and their role in presenting the Sunnah. Then there follows a discussion about the importance of reason and its role in understanding Islamic beliefs, values and practical laws.

The second chapter studies fundamental doctrines of Islam i.e. unity of God, prophethood and resurrection which constitute the principles of religion for Islam and other divine religions. In this chapter there is also a discussion about some of the doctrinal differences among Muslims on issues such as the *imamate*.

The third chapter is a very brief account of Islamic practices along with brief references to the objectives and principles underlying them. These practices are in principle shared by all Muslims, though there may be some differences in particulars among different Islamic schools.

The fourth chapter studies some aspects of Islamic moral system and ends with reference to some of the outcomes of living a life of faith along with significance of supplication.

The fifth and final chapter is a short discussion about the Muslim world today. This chapter starts with a brief account of the latest statistics about the present Muslim population of the world and goes on with a brief study of holy cities for Muslims.

In conclusion I would like to take this opportunity to thank all the individuals and organisations that have encouraged me and supported publishing this book, especially Islamic Centre of England, London. Last but certainly not least, I would like to express my feelings of deep gratitude to God for all His favours that He has bestowed upon us in the past and in the present.

Mohammad A. Shomali
London, June 2007

Chapter 1
SOURCES OF ISLAMIC THOUGHT

Before studying Islamic doctrines or practices, it is necessary to know the sources on which Muslims rely for understanding Islam. In what follows, we will study major sources of Islamic thought, on which any investigation about Islam has to be based: the Glorious Qur'an, the Sunnah and reason.

The Glorious Qur'an

Needless to say, the Qur'an is the most important source for all Muslims. The Qur'an also acts as an instrument of unity among all Muslims. Regardless of their different sectarian and cultural backgrounds, all Muslims refer to the same Book as the divine guide to govern their life.

Muslims deny any alteration in the Qur'an and believe that the Qur'an available today is the same that was revealed to the Prophet Muhammad. No one has ever seen a copy of the Qur'an different from the standard one in any part of the Islamic world. There are manuscripts of the Qur'an available today that go back to the time of early Islam and they are exactly the same as the current ones.

The Glorious Qur'an itself explicitly says that God Himself preserves the Qur'an from any distortion or loss:

> Surely We have revealed the Reminder and We will most surely be its preserver. (15:9)

Regarding this verse, 'Allamah Tabataba'i in his renowned *Al-Mizan fi Tafsir al-Qur'an*, one of the greatest commentaries of the Qur'an, states:

> ...the Qur'an is a living and eternal Reminder which will never die and fall into oblivion. It is immune from any addition and loss. It is immune from and secure against any alterations in form and style which could affect its character and role as "the Reminder of Allah which expresses divine truth and knowledge". For this reason, the aforesaid verse indicates that the divine Book has always been and will continue to be guarded against any distortion and alteration.[1]

The Sunnah

After the Glorious Qur'an, the most important source for understanding Islam is the Sunnah of the Prophet Muhammad, including his sayings and his deeds. The Qur'an itself grants this high position to the Prophet, as he is referred to as the one who is responsible for purifying people and teaching them the Qur'an and wisdom (62:2). The Prophet is a perfect role model for the believers (33:21). He never speaks out of his own wishes (53:3). Muslims are asked to hold on to whatever he gives them and refrain from whatever he prohibits (59:7).

---

[1] *Al-Mizan fi Tafsir al-Qur'an*, Vol. 12, p. 99.

Knowing the above verses and many other verses regarding the status of the Prophet, and taking into account the significance of being a divine messenger chosen directly by God, Muslims have cultivated a state of sincere love for and devotion to the Prophet Muhammad.

Muslims see in the Prophet Muhammad the perfect model of entire reliance on God, profound knowledge of God, ultimate devotion to God, sincere obedience to the divine Will, the noblest of character, and compassion and mercy for all mankind. It was not accidental that he was chosen by God to deliver His final message for humanity. To be able to receive divine revelation and be addressed by God requires possession of a very high calibre. Naturally to be able to receive the most perfect revelation requires the highest calibre.

The personal character and behaviour of the Prophet contributed greatly to the progress of Islam. He was known to be an honest, trustworthy and pious person from childhood. During his prophethood, he always lived by his principles and values. In the times of ease as well as difficulty, security as well as fear, peace as well as war, victory as well as defeat, he always manifested humility, justice and confidence. He was so humble that he never admired himself, he never felt superior to others and he never lived a life of luxury. Both when he was alone and powerless as well as when he ruled the Arab peninsula and Muslims were whole-heartedly following him, he behaved the same. He lived very simply and was always with the people, especially the poor. He had no palace or guard. When he was sitting with his companions no one could distinguish him from others by considering his seat or clothes. It was only his words and spirituality that distinguished him from others.

He was so just that he never ignored the rights of anyone, even his enemies. He exemplified in his life the Qur'anic command, "O you who believe! Be upright for God, bearers of witness with justice, and let not hatred of a people incite you not to act equitably; act equitably, that is nearer to piety" (5:8).

Before battles, he always gave instructions to his soldiers not to harm women, children, the elderly, and those who had surrendered, not to destroy farms and gardens, not to chase those who had escaped from the war front, and to be kind to their captives.

Just before his demise, the Prophet announced in the Mosque: "Whoever among you feels that I have done injustice to him, come forward and do justice. Surely, enacting justice in this world is better in my view than being taken account of in the Hereafter in front of the angels and the Prophets."

Those present in the Mosque wept, for they were reminded of all the sacrifices that the Prophet had made for them and the troubles that he had undergone in order to guide them. They knew that he never gave any priority to his own needs and never preferred his comfort and convenience to others. They therefore responded with statements of deep gratitude and profound respect. But one among them, Sawadah b. Qays, stood up and said: "May my father and mother be your ransom! O Messenger of God! On your return from Ta'if, I came to welcome you while you were riding your camel. You raised your stick to direct your camel, but the stick struck my stomach. I do not know whether this strike was intentional or unintentional." The Prophet replied: "I seek refuge from God from having done so intentionally."

The Prophet then asked Bilal to go to the house of Fatimah and bring the same stick. After the stick was brought, the Prophet told Sawadah to retaliate by hitting him back. Sawadah said that the stick had struck the skin of his stomach. The Prophet therefore lifted his shirt so that Sawadah could in return strike his skin. At that moment, Sawadah asked: "O Messenger of God! Do you allow me to touch my mouth to your stomach?" The Prophet gave him permission. Sawadah then kissed the stomach of the Prophet and prayed that because of this act of his, God would protect him from fire on the Day of Resurrection. The Prophet said: "O Sawadah! Will you pardon me or do you still wish to retaliate?" He replied: "I pardon you." The Prophet then prayed: "O God! Pardon Sawadah b. Qays as he pardoned Your Prophet, Muhammad!"[1]

The household of the Prophet

There seems to be no disagreement among Muslims about the validity of following the teachings of the household of the Prophet in understanding Islam, especially if we note that according to the Sunni view all the companions of the Prophet were reliable sources of understanding Islam.[2] This fact becomes even clearer when we refer to the traditions from the Prophet about his household, and examine sayings

---

[1] *Mustadrak Wasa'il al-Shi'ah*, Vol. 18, pp. 287 & 288.

[2] Sunni Muslims hold that whoever met the Prophet while believing in him is considered as a companion of the Prophet and can be relied on in acquiring knowledge about Islam. Accordingly, members of the household of the Prophet such as Imam Ali and Fatimah who were always with the Prophet and had the closest relation to the Prophet can unquestionably be relied on.

of Sunni scholars about the knowledge of Ali and other members of the household of the Prophet.[1]

One of the most well-known traditions about the stauts of Ahlul Bayt is the tradition of *Thaqalayn*. This tradition was uttered by the Prophet on different occasions, including the day of 'Arafah and the 18th of *Dhu'l-Hijjah* in Ghadir Khum in his last pilgrimage. Despite minor differences in the wording the essence remains the same in all versions of the tradition. For example, in one version of the tradition the Prophet said:

> Oh people! I leave among you two precious things: the Book of God and my household. As long as you hold on to them you will not go astray.

Or in another tradition the Prophet said:

> I leave among you two precious things, which if you hold on to you will not go astray after me: the Book of God which is like a rope extended between the heaven and the earth, and my household. These two things will not separate from each other until they reach me near the fountain on the Day of Judgement. Take care in how you treat them after me.

---

[1] For example, Imam Malik says: "No eyes have ever seen, no ears have ever heard, and nothing has ever come to the heart of any human being better than Ja'far b. Muhammad, who is distinguished in his knowledge, his piety, his asceticism, and in his servitude to God." This is what Ibn Taymiyah reports from Imam Malik in his book *Al-Tawassul wa al-Wasilah*, p. 52, first edition.

This shows that the Prophet was worried about the way that Muslims, or at least some of them, would treat the Qur'an and his household. In another tradition he said:

> I leave two successors: first, the Book of God which is like a rope extended between heaven and the earth, and second, my household. They will not separate from each other until they come to me near the fountain of Kawthar.

The above traditions can be found in major Sunni sources, such as: *Sahih* of Muslim (Vol. 8, p. 25, No. 2408), *Musnad* of Imam Ahmad (Vol. 3, p. 388, No. 10720), *Sunan* of Darimi (Vol. 2, p. 432), and *Sahih* of Tirmidhi (Vol. 5, p. 6432, No. 3788). They are also mentioned in books such as *Usd al-Ghabah* by Ibn Athir (Vol. 2, p. 13), *Al-Sunan al-Kubra* by Bayhaqi (Vol. 2, p. 198) and *Kanz al-'Ummal* (Vol. 1, p. 44).

This hadith in all versions indicates that:

- From the time of the Prophet until the end of the world the Book of God and the household of the Prophet will always be together.

- No one can say that the book of God is enough, and that we do not need the household of the Prophet, or vice versa, for the Prophet clearly said: I leave two precious things that you must grasp and if you do so you will not be misled.

- The household of the Prophet would never make mistakes and they are always truthful.

- It is also interesting that according to this hadith the household of the Prophet, like the Qur'an itself, is held to be persistent until the Day of Judgement. Thus, the household of the Prophet will never disappear, even for a short period of time.

The other hadith is the hadith of *Safinah* (ship). All Muslims have narrated that the Prophet said:

> "Be aware that surely the example of my household among you is like the example of the ship of Noah. Whoever boarded the ship of Noah was saved and whoever refused to enter the ship of Noah was drowned."

The hadith of *Safinah* in its different versions emphasises the same fact and can be found in *Mustadrak* by Hakim Nishaburi, Vol. 3, pp. 149 & 151, *Arba'in Hadith* by Nabahani, *al-Sawa'iq al-Muhriqah* by Ibn Hajar amongst other sources.

Thus, according to these sets of traditions the appeal to the guidance of the household of the Prophet is of the utmost necessity.

Note: The tradition of *thaqalayn* is mentioned in both Sunni and Shi'a sources so it is a matter of agreement among all Muslims. However, there is a version of the hadith (narrated only in some sources) in which the Prophet is quoted as saying 'my Sunnah' instead of 'my household'. Provided that this version too can be authenticated, the result would be that as one side of the comparison is the same, i.e. the Qur'an, the other side too must be identical; otherwise there would be no consistency in what has been narrated from the Prophet has said. Thus, the very act of referring to the teachings and advice of the household of the Prophet is the very act of referring to the Sunnah of the Prophet. This means that to reach the Sunnah of the Prophet and to understand exactly what his Sunnah was, one needs to refer to his household who have had the closest relationship with him and who knew better than anyone else what he said or did or approved.[1]

Who constitute the household of the Prophet?

According to many traditions, we are told to refer to the household of the Prophet: *"Ahlul Bayt"* or *"Itrah"*. What do these terms refer to? There is no doubt among Muslims that certainly Fatimah, the daughter of the Prophet, Imam Ali, and their sons Imam Hasan and Imam Husayn are members of his household. The only concern is whether other relatives of the Prophet are included or not, and if so, to what extent. Of course, everyone must accept that Ahlul Bayt exclude those who did not embrace Islam, such as Abu Lahab, one of the uncles of the Prophet and at the same time one of his enemies who is cursed in the Qur'an. Ahlul Bayt are those who have proportionate levels of faith and knowledge that make it possible for them to be mentioned along with the Qur'an in the tradition of the *Thaqalayn*. Interestingly the Prophet himself has clearly defined who the Ahlul Bayt are.

In what follows, I will mention some hadiths narrated in major Sunni sources:

(1) Muslim narrates from 'Ayishah, *Umm al-Mu'minin* that the The Prophet went out wearing a black woollen cloak, when Hasan the son of Ali came to him, so the Prophet let Hasan come in with him under the cloak. Then Husayn came and he too entered. Then Fatimah came. She entered as well. Then Ali came. He also went under the cloak, such

---

[1] Whatever Ahlul Bayt taught was exactly what they had themselves received from the Prophet. There are many traditions in this regard. For example, in *Usul al-Kafi* we find that Imam Sadiq said that whatever he said was what he had received through his forefathers from the Prophet.

that the cloak covered the Prophet, Ali, Fatimah, Hasan and Husayn. Then the Prophet recited:

> God only desires to keep away impurity from you, O People of the House! And to purify you a (thorough) purification (33:33).[1]

(2) Muslim narrates from Sa'd b. Abi Waqqas that he was asked by Mu'awiyah why he refused to verbally abuse Ali. Sa'd replied:

> I remember three sayings of the Prophet about Ali which caused me not to say anything bad about him. If I possessed even one of these qualities it would be better for me than red camels.[2] The first was that when the Prophet wanted to go to the war of Tabuk, he left Ali in Medina. Ali was very sad at not having the good fortune to join the army and fight for the sake of God. He went to the Prophet, saying: 'Do you leave me with children and women?' The Prophet replied: 'Are you not happy to be to me as Aaron was to Moses, except that there will be no prophet after me?' Second I heard from the Prophet on the day of conquest of Khaybar: 'Certainly I will give the flag [of Islam] to a man that loves God and His Messenger and is loved by God and His Messenger'. We hoped to be given the flag, but the Prophet said: 'Call Ali for me!' Ali came while suffering from pain in his eyes. The Prophet gave him the flag and at his

---

[1] *Sahih* of Muslim, Vol. 4, p. 1883, No. 2424. (Kitab Fada'il al-Sahabah, Bab Fada'il Ahlul Bayt, Sakhr serial no. 4450)

[2] Red camels were very valuable at the time.

hands God granted us victory. Third when the verse of Mubahalah was revealed the Prophet called Ali, Fatimah, Hasan and Husayn and said: 'My Lord! These are my household'. [1]

(3) Imam Ahmad b. Hanbal narrates from Anas b. Malik that when the verse of *tathir* (33:33) was revealed, for six months the Prophet used to call at the house of Ali and Fatimah every morning on his way to the mosque for the Dawn Prayer and say:

> Prayer, O People of the House! 'God only desires to keep away impurity from you, O People of the House! And to purify you a (thorough) purification' (33:33).[2]

Reason

Reason is a reliable source of knowledge and in complete harmony with revelation. According to some hadiths, God has two proofs (*hujjah*), through which humans can understand His will: the internal one which is reason (*al-'aql*) and the external, which are the Prophets. Sometimes reason is called, "the internal Prophet" and the Prophets are called "the external reason". There is an established rule that whatever judgement is made by reason is the same as that made by the religion (*shar'*) and vice versa. It is also unanimously accepted that one of the conditions of moral or legal responsibility is to have sound reason. If someone is insane, he is not considered as responsible for his actions.

---

[1] *Sahih* of Muslim, Vol. 4, p. 1871, no. 2408. (Kitab Fada'il al-Sahabah, Sakhr serial No. 4420).

[2] *Musnad* of Imam Ahmad b. Hanbal, Sakhr serial no. 13231. See also *Sunan* of al-Tirmidhi, Sakhr serial no. 3130.

What is expected of the people in religion also varies according to their mental and rational capacity. Those who are very clever and intelligent are expected to be more prepared, pious, and obedient than those who are not.

According to the Qur'an, God requires all human beings to exercise their rational faculty and to ponder on His signs and communications in the universe. On many occasions disbelievers are condemned because of their failure to think or to act according to rational requirements. For example, they are condemned because of their blind imitation of their ancestors, and there are many verses with rhetorical questions, such as: "Do not they think?!" (36:68), "Do not they ponder on the Qur'an?!" (4:82; 47:24) and "In these, there are signs for those who are thoughtful" (13:4; 16:67; 30:28).

In general, reason contributes to religious studies in three major areas: The first is in understanding the realities of the world, such as the existence of God, the truth of religion and scientific facts. The second is in introducing principles of moral values and legal norms, such as the evil of oppression and the good of justice. The third is in setting up standards and logical processes of reasoning and inference. All these three roles of reason are recognised and, indeed, recommended by Islam.

In contrast, the role of revelation or the Scriptures in religious studies can be summed up as follows:

- ➢ confirmation of the facts that are already known by reason;

- ➢ introducing new subjects that are not known by reason, such as details of resurrection and detailed accounts of moral and legal systems;

> providing sanctions through the religious system of reward and punishment.

To conclude I should mention that there is nothing irrational in Islam. Of course, one has to distinguish between certain and decisive rational judgements, and one's guessing or personal opinions. If there is a case in which it seems that rational judgement is in conflict with certain religious positions, one has to accept that there must be a mistake in at least one side: either it was not a real judgement of reason or it was not a religious law. God never misleads people by telling them to do something through the Prophets, and the opposite thing through our God-given reason. There have always been some judgements attributed to reason and taken as contradicting religious positions that after close consideration have proven to be contrary to decisive rational premises.

It has to be noted that every scholar has to refer directly to the above sources of Islam. One cannot beg the question just by accepting what has been said by previous generations. View of other people or scholars or even their consensus *by itself* is not sufficient as a proof; just as one person may make mistake, two, three, or thousands, or even all of them may do so. However, whenever there exists an agreement among all Muslims or Muslim scholars in a way whereby the agreement unveils the Sunnah, it can serve as a proof, as an instrument to uncover the will of God. For example, when we find that every Muslim in the time of the Prophet said his prayer in a certain way we realize that the Prophet had instructed them to do so; otherwise there would be no factor to unify their action. It is not possible to imagine that they all had acted blindly and without instruction, or that they all made mistakes and the Prophet did not correct them.

Thus, consensus in itself is not a proof. It only works when it leads to the discovery of the Sunnah. Accordingly, if Muslims today agree on a given subject, while a scholar has doubt about the Islamic judgement on that subject, he methodologically cannot say that because everybody says so, I also say the same. There have been many cases in the history where all human beings believed in the same way and later they found out that they were wrong, e.g. the earth being flat. It is only the Qur'an and the Sunnah that are unquestionably true and immune from any error or mistake. This approach grants a type of dynamism to Islamic thought, so that every generation of scholars and even any single scholar is able and indeed is required to refer directly to the Qur'an and The Sunnah and conduct his own original *ijtihād*, that is his investigation and independent judgement. The view of no jurist, however high his position, is immune from scientific questioning or challenge. Of course, as in any other discipline, every religious scholar needs to consult and examine carefully the works of his predecessors.

Chapter 2
DOCTRINES

Throughout the history of Islam, Muslims, in spite of their differences, have had a great deal of agreement, not only on principles of Islam, but also on many practices. The Qur'an and the great personality of the Prophet on the one hand, and the sincere love and devotion of all Muslims towards them on the other, have unified Muslims and made out of them a real nation that has its own identity, heritage, civilization, aims, objectives and destiny. The hostility of the enemies of Islam, along with the challenges of the age, has also strengthened the sense of unity and brotherhood among Muslims. The Qur'anic and prophetic call for unity and brotherhood has always been echoed by great leading Islamic personalities of different schools of Islam.

With respect to beliefs, all Muslims share the belief in God and His unity, mercy and justice, the Prophets in general and the mission of the Prophet Muhammad in particular, the Resurrection, and the just and equal treatment of everybody on the Day of Judgement. These are the most fundamental principles of Islam which are agreed upon by all Muslims. An outside view about the extent of the agreement between Shi'a and Sunni Muslims is expressed in the following passage:

> Since the Iranian Revolution everyone knows that Shi'ites are Muslims, like the Sunnis respecting the central dogma of the oneness of

God, the same sacred writing (the Koran), the same Prophet Mohammad, the same belief in the resurrection followed by the last Judgement and the same fundamental obligations, prayer, fasting, pilgrimage, almsgiving, and jihād (holy war). These common points are more important than the differences: there is no longer any theoretical objection to a Shi'ite performing his prayers with a Sunni, or vice versa although many difficulties have existed in the past and in practice still remain.[1]

In what follows, we will proceed by outlining principles of religion or articles of faith.[2]

Unity of God

The Islamic faith is formulated by the declaration of two facts, i.e. that there is no god (i.e. no one worthy of worship) but God (*Allah*) and that Muhammad is His messenger (*LĀ ILĀHA ILLALLĀH MUHAMMADUR- RASŪLULLĀH*). Muslims believe that God is ONE. He has no partner or children. He is the Beginning and He is the End. He is Omnipotent, Omniscient and Omnipresent. The Qur'an says that He is closer to man than his jugular vein, but He cannot be seen by eyes or encompassed by human intellect. In a supplication, Imam Ali says:

> Oh God, verily I ask Thee by Thy Name, in the name of Allah, the All-merciful, the All-

---

[1] Richard, *Shi'ite Islam*, 1995, p. 5 (with abbreviation).

[2] One of the sources of the following discussions on the principles and practices of Islam is "An Introduction to Islam" by the late Bashir Rahim. For this and other introductions to Islam, see www.al-islam.org.

compassionate, O the Possessor of Majesty and Splendour, the Living, the Self-subsistent, the Eternal, there is no god other than Thee.

Divine justice

Among divine attributes, historically great emphasis has been put on justice. God is just (*'ādil*), in the sense that God never commits any injustice towards His servants, and He never oppresses anyone. This fact is clearly expressed by the Qur'an. For example, we read:

> God is not in the least unjust to the servants. (3:182 & 8:51 & 22:10)

> Surely God does not do any injustice to people, but people are unjust to themselves. (10:44)

Underlying the doctrine of divine justice is the idea that good and bad or right and wrong are objective and rational. For example, honesty is objectively different from dishonesty and it can be rationally understood that while honesty is a virtue, dishonesty is bad. One does not need to be a religious person to understand basic moral principles such as goodness of honesty. Thus, it becomes clear that it was not arbitrary that God has commanded us to be just and not to oppress anyone, even our enemies.

This emphasis on the issue of divine justice has not been limited to the theoretical aspect of Islam. God treats human beings with justice and wants them to deal with each other justly and establish justice in the society. Indeed, the issue of justice occupies a very fundamental position in Muslim practice and call for the implementation of the principle of justice always remains as the first agenda in any social reform. All the Prophets were sent to establish social justice:

> We have sent Our messengers with clear proofs, and sent the Book and the Balance down along with them, so that mankind may establish social justice. (57:25)
>
> Surely God commands justice, benevolence and giving to the kindred.(16:90)

It is a universal duty for everyone to implement justice both in his individual and social life. A Muslim is the one who is just to himself,[1] to his spouse and children,[2] and to everybody else, including one's enemies.[3] According to Shi'a jurisprudence, there are many religious or socio-political positions that require the position holder to be just. For example, Imams of the daily prayers who lead the congregations, Friday prayer leaders, witnesses, judges, religious authorities and political leaders all must be just.

Prophethood

God has created mankind for a purpose (51:56). He has given man reason and free-will to find his way towards his perfection and happiness. He has also supplemented the human reason with divine revelation. Through His wisdom and justice, He has not left any people or corner of the

---

[1] In the Islamic worldview, whoever disobeys God has oppressed himself. The Qur'an says: "whoever breaks divine laws has oppressed himself". (65:1)

[2] According to a hadith, similar to which there are many others: "Surely God does not get angry for anything as much as He gets angry for the women and children (being oppressed)".

[3] Muslims are required to deal with justice and fairness even with their enemies. The Qur'an says: "Do not let your hostility towards some people to make you unjust. Be just. Justice is closer to the piety." (5:8)

world without guidance; He has sent Prophets to all nations to instruct and guide them (10:47 and 16:36).

The first Prophet was Adam and the last was Muhammad (33:40). The Qur'an mentions twenty-five of the Prophets by their names and states that there were many more (40:78). Through the indications of hadiths, Muslims believe that there have been 124,000 Prophets. Amongst those mentioned in the Qur'an are Adam, Noah, Abraham, Ishmael, Isaac, Lot, Jacob, Joseph, Job, Moses, Aaron, Ezekiel, David, Solomon, Jonah, Zachariah, John the Baptist, Jesus and Muhammad. Among them, Noah, Abraham, Moses, Jesus and Muhammad are believed to be the greatest. They are called, "*Ulū'l-'Azm*" meaning those of great determination.

Other than itself, the Qur'an speaks of four Heavenly books: the Book of Abraham (87:19); the Psalms of David (4:163 and 17:55); the Torah of Moses (2:87, 3:3 & 4, 6:91 & 154) and the Gospel of Jesus (5:46).

A Muslim must believe in all the Holy Books (2:4 & 285) and in all the Prophets (4:152). As we will see later, the Shi'a also believe that all the Prophets were necessarily infallible and sinless prior to and during their mission.

Imāmah

The Shi'a view: The Shi'a believe in the institution of Imāmah as successorship to prophethood. In Arabic the term "Imām" literally means "leader". An Imam, in general terminology, may be good or bad, and the extent of his leadership may be very broad, such as leading a whole nation, or limited such as leading prayers in a mosque. However, in the Shi'i faith the Imam in its narrower sense is the person who is in charge of all political and religious affairs of the Islamic nation. More exactly, the Imam is the person who is appointed by God and introduced by the Prophet and then by each preceding Imam by explicit designation (*nass*) to lead the Muslim community, interpret and protect the religion and the law (*shari'ah*), and guide the community in their affairs. The Imam must be sinless and possess divine knowledge of both the exoteric and the esoteric meaning of the Qur'an.

The Twelver Shi'a who constitute the vast majority of Shi'a Muslims believe that the Prophet was succeeded by twelve Imams.[1] These are:

1. Imam Ali b. Abi Talib[2]   Martyred 40/659
2. Imam Hasan b. Ali   Martyred 50/669
3. Imam Husayn b. Ali   Martyred 61/680
4. Imam Ali b. Husayn   Martyred 95/712

---

[1] There is a series of hadiths, in which the prophet mentioned that there would be twelve leaders after him. For example, Bukhari reports that the Prophet said: "There will be twelve leaders (*amir*) after me." Then the narrator says that the Prophet said something that he could not hear. He asked his father, who too was present at the time, to tell him what the Prophet had said. His father said that the Prophet had said: "All these twelve leaders will be from the tribe of Quraysh." (*Sahih* of Bukhari, Kitab al-Ahkam, Chapter 51 on al-Istikhlaf) Muslim also reports this tradition, saying that the narrator of this tradition went with his father to the place where the Prophet was, and the Prophet said: "This religion will not end until there will have been twelve successors (*khalifah*)". Then the narrator says: "The Prophet said something I did not understand and I asked my father. He said, the Prophet said: 'They are all from Quraysh'." (*Sahih* of Muslim, Kitab al-Imarah, Chapter: the people follow Quraysh and that caliphate is in Quraysh)

[2] Imam Ali was the Prophet's cousin and son-in-law (the husband of the Lady Fatimah). He was the first man who embraced Islam.

5. Imam Muhammad b. Ali	Martyred 114/732.
6. Imam Ja'far b. Muhammad	Martyred 148/765
7. Imam Musa b. Ja'far	Martyred 183/799
8. Imam Ali b. Musa	Martyred 203/817
9. Imam Muhammad b. Ali	Martyred 220/835
10. Imam Ali b. Muhammad	Martyred 254/868
11. Imam Hasan b. Ali	Martyred 260/872
12. **Imam al-Mahdi**	Born 255/868.

The Sunni View: Sunni Muslims use the term Imam as an equivalent to the term "Caliph" (*khalifah*). In Arabic the term "khalifah" means successor. The term has been used as a title for whoever took the power and ruled the Islamic state after the demise of the Prophet Muhammad. A Caliph may be elected, or nominated by his predecessor, or selected by a committee, or may even acquire power through military force. A Caliph need not be sinless. Neither does he need to be the most knowledgeable or the most pious.

Saviour: The belief in a saviour is shared by most (if not all) religions. In Islam, the idea of a saviour is very deliberately presented in the doctrine of al-Mahdi (the Guided) who will rise up with divine blessing and fill the earth with justice after it has been filled with injustice and oppression. The idea of a saviour or a good end for the world is indicated in many Qur'anic verses and Islamic hadiths. For example, we read in the Qur'an:

> We have written in the Psalms following the Reminder: "My honourable servants shall inherit the earth" (21:105).

Yet we wanted to endow those who were considered inferior on earth, and make them into leaders and make them [Our] heirs (28:5).

The following are only some examples of hadiths on the idea of the saviour narrated in both Sunni and Shi'a sources:

1. The Prophet said:

> Even if the entire duration of the world's existence has already been exhausted and only one day is left (before the day of judgment), God will expand that day to such a length of time, as to accommodate the kingdom of a person from my household who will be called by my name.[1]

2. The Prophet also said:

> **Al-Mahdi** is one of us, the members of the household (Ahlul Bayt). God will prepare for him (his affairs) in one night.[2]

3. Furthermore, the Prophet said:

---

[1] *Sunan* of al-Tirmidhi, Kitab al-Fitan, Sakhr serial no. 2156 & 2157 and *Sunan* of Abu Dawud, Kitab al-Mahdi, serial no. 3733 & 3734. According to Abu Dawud, the hadith ends with, "He will fill out the earth with justice as it will have been full of injustice and oppression." See also *Musnad* of Ahmad, Musnad al-'Asharah al-Mubashsharin bi al-Jannah, serial no. 734 and *Sunan* of Ibn Majah, Kitab al- Jihād, serial no. 2769.

[2] *Sunan* of Ibn Majah, Kitab al-Fitan, Sakhr serial no. 4075 and *Musnad* of Ahmad, Musnad al-'Asharah al-Mubashsharin bi al-Jannah, serial no. 610.

Al-Mahdi will be of my family, of the descendants of Fatimah.[1]

Al-Mahdi will have a universal mission. He will fill the earth with justice after being filled with injustice and oppression. He will be accompanied by Jesus.[2] His name will be the same as the name of the Prophet Muhammad and he will be from the progeny of the Lady Fatimah.

The Shi'a view: The Shi'a believe that Mahdi is the son of Imam Hasan al-'Askari. He was born in 255 (A.H). His occultation began in the year 260 (A.H). He is still alive, but protected by God in the state of occultation till preparations are made for his reappearance.

The Sunni view: Most Sunni scholars believe that Mahdi has not yet been born. However, there have been many who believed that Mahdi was the son of Imam Hasan and already born. For example, one may refer to Muhammad b. Yousuf al-Kanjī al-Shafi'ī in his *Al-Bayān fī Akhbār Sāhib al-Zamān* and *Kifāyat al-Tālib fī Manāqib Ali b. Abī Tālib*; Nūr al-Dīn Ali b. Muhammad al-Mālikī in his *Al-Fusūl al-Muhimmah fī Ma'rifat al-A'immah* and Ibn al-Jawzī in his well-known *Tadhkirat al-Khawāss*.

Resurrection

This world will come to an end. Then on the Day of the Resurrection (*Qiyāmah*) all people will be resurrected and presented before God who will decide their individual fates

---

[1] *Sunan* of Abu Dawud, Kitab al-Mahdi, Sakhr serial no. 3735. See also *Sunan* of Ibn Majah, Kitab al-Fitan, Sakhr serial no. 4076.

[2] For example, see *Sahih* of Muslim, Kitab al-Iman, Sakhr serial no. 225 and *Musnad* of Ahmad, Baqi Musnad al-Mukthirin, Sakhr serial no. 14193 & 14595.

according to their beliefs and deeds in this world. Good will be rewarded and evil be punished (22:1, 2 & 6-9; 3:185; 6:62). God will treat people with justice but the dominant factor in the administration of His Justice will be His Mercy (6:12).

Note

Although all Muslims believe in the above principles of Islam, there is a slight difference in their articulation of Islamic beliefs and practices.

Sunni view: Sunni Muslims usually present the declaration of Islam (*kalimah*) consisting of bearing witness that there is no god but God (*Allah*) and that Muhammad is His Messenger together with four acts of worship, i.e. the daily prayer, fasting, pilgrimage to Mecca and almsgiving as the Five Pillars of Faith. They consider other acts of worship such as enjoining good and forbidding evil, and struggle in the way of God as obligatory acts that are not included amongst the Pillars of Faith.

Shi'a view: Shi'a Muslims express the above beliefs as principles or roots of the religion (*Usūl al-Dīn*) and the acts of worship to follow as practices or branches of the religion (*Furū' al-Dīn*). The reason for such an articulation is that those beliefs are the most fundamental aspects of the religion and the criteria for being considered a Muslim. However, the mandatory acts of worship are implications of being faithful, since genuine faith manifests itself in practices. Due to the ultimate importance of the notion of divine justice for any value system and the notion of imamate in successorship to the Prophet, the Shi'a have frequently introduced them along with unity of God, prophethood, and resurrection as five Principles of the Faith (*Usūl al-Madhhab*) in contrast to unity of God, prophethood and resurrection which count as the three Principles of Religion (*Uṣūl al-Dīn*), which are shared by all followers of the Abrahamic faiths.

Chapter 3
PRACTICES

The main mandatory acts of worship in Islam are as follows:

1. The Daily Prayers

Every Muslim from the time he or she attains puberty must perform five daily prayers (*salāt*). To be able to begin the prayer one must first perform the ritual ablution (*wudū*) in the prescribed form. Then, one stands facing Mecca and makes an intention to perform the specific prayer of the time in order to attain proximity to God. This intention must be kept at all times during the prayer. If someone forgets what he is doing, or prays in order to show off, or for any other selfish motive, his prayer becomes void. The actual prayer starts when the person utters: *Allāh-u Akbar* (God is the Greatest). With this he enters the formal state of prayer in which he remains until the completion of his prayers.

Each prayer consists of two to four units (*rak'ah*).[1] Each unit consists of:

---

[1] The morning prayer (*fajr*) which is performed between dawn and sunrise consists of two units, the noon (*zuhr*) and afternoon prayers (*'asr*) each consist of four units, the sunset prayer (*maghrib*) consists of three units and the evening (*'ishā'*) consists of four units.

i. reciting the opening chapter of the Qur'an and another chapter such as *Tawhīd* or *Qadr*;[1]

ii. bowing down (*rukū'*) and praising and glorifying God in that position;

iii. performing two prostrations (*sajdah*) and then praising and glorifying God.

The prayers are ended by bearing witness that God is One and has no partners and that Muhammad is His servant and messenger with salutations upon him and his household (*tashahhud*) and offering peace to the Prophet, all the righteous people, and all who are engaged in prayers (*taslīm*).

The daily prayer is the most important form of worship and remembrance of the Lord. The Qur'an says:

> Surely prayer keeps (one) away from indecency and evil, and certainly the remembrance of God is greater, and God knows what you do. (29:45)

2. Fasting

The second act of worship is fasting (*sawm*) during the month of Ramadan, the ninth month of the Islamic calendar. In this month, Muslims refrain from eating, drinking and sexual activity with their spouses from dawn to

---

[1] In three unit and four unit prayers the third and fourth units consist first of recitation of the opening chapter of the Qur'an, or alternatively, recitation of a specific remembrance (*dhikr*) called, "*al-tasbīḥāt al-arbi'ah*" (Four Glorifications) and then bowing down and prostrations. In these prayers the affirmation of the oneness of God and the prophethood of the Prophet Muhammad and salutations upon him and his household are performed in both the second unit and the last unit after prostrations.

sunset.[1] Like any other acts of worship, fasting must be performed with pure intention, that is, solely for the sake of God and to attain proximity to Him. Along with closeness to God and achieving His pleasure, fasting has many other benefits, such as strengthening one's determination, reminding people of God's blessings which they may take for granted, such as the food that they enjoy everyday, remembering the hunger and thirst of the Day of Judgement, helping the rich to understand what the poor experience in order to awaken their sense of benevolence and sympathy, weakening one's appetites and lower desires, and letting rational understanding and spiritual awareness flourish. The Qur'an says:

> O you who believe! Fasting is prescribed for you, as it was prescribed for those before you, so that you may guard (against evil). (2:183)

3. Pilgrimage to Mecca

Every Muslim who has attained puberty, and is financially and physically capable, must once perform pilgrimage to Mecca (*hajj*) in the month of *Dhu'l-Hijjah*, the twelfth month of the Islamic calendar. The most important Mosque for Muslims all over the world is called *Masjid al-Harām*, which is the sanctuary of the *Ka'bah*, and is located in Mecca.

All Muslims face towards the Ka'bah in their prayers. The Ka'bah is the cubical construction built by the Prophet Abraham and his son, Prophet Ishmael, on the foundations of what had originally been built by the Prophet Adam. Indeed, to a great extent, pilgrimage to Mecca is a symbolic

---

[1] Several groups of people are exempted from fasting, such as the sick or those who travel. Details are to be learnt from jurisprudencial books.

reconstruction of what the Prophet Abraham, the arch monotheist went through in that very place about four thousand years ago. After a long journey, when Abraham arrived in Mecca he was asked by God to make preparations for pilgrims going to Mecca. The Qur'an says:

> Do not associate with Me anything, and purify My house for those who circle around it and stand to pray and bow and prostrate themselves. And proclaim among the people the pilgrimage. They will come to you on foot and on every lean camel from every remote path so that they may witness the benefits for them; and mention the name of God during the appointed days over what He has given them (22:26-28).

> Most surely the first house appointed for men is the one at Bekka (Mecca), blessed and a guidance for the nations. In it are clear signs, the standing place of Abraham, and whoever enters it shall be secure. Pilgrimage to the House is incumbent upon people for the sake of God, (upon) everyone who is able to undertake the journey to it; and whoever turns away, then surely God is Self-sufficient, above any need of the worlds (3:96 & 97).

Pilgrimage to Mecca is full of unforgettable experiences. Among them, perhaps the most outstanding are selflessness, brotherhood, equality and simplicity. Every year millions of Muslims from different continents leave their home, family, business, and whatever else is dear to them, and set out on their journey towards Mecca, located in a desert. Everyone is asked to be present there in the same places at the same time all wearing the same clothes and performing the same rites. The rich and the poor, the king and the ordinary man, the elite and the layman all stand shoulder to shoulder and wear two pieces of white cloth. This is something that everyone must experience at least once in his lifetime, and should then try to implement lessons learnt from the experience in his day to day life.

4. Almsgiving

Giving charity is highly recommended in the Qur'an and The Sunnah and the reward for charitable acts is great. Although everything including one's financial possessions belongs to God in reality, the Qur'an presents giving charity as offering a loan to God:

> Who is the one that lends to God a good lending so that God may give him double? (57:11)

In addition to voluntary charities, there are certain types of charity that are obligatory. For example, one type of almsgiving is *zakāt*, a wealth tax of a small percentage (usually 2.5%). Paying zakāt is not a gift for the poor but rather is their due right that must be observed:

> And in their properties is the right of the beggar and the destitute (51:19).

Imam Ali also said:

> God the Glorified has fixed the livelihood of the destitute in the wealth of the rich. Consequently, whenever the destitute remains hungry, it is because some rich persons have denied him his share.[1]

---

[1] *Nahj al-Balāghah*, edited by Fayd al-Islam, Wise-saying 320.

Those whose possessions of certain amounts of wheat, barley, dates, raisins, gold, silver, camels, cows and sheep surpass certain quantities must pay zakāt on a yearly basis to the less fortunate amongst their relatives, the orphans, the needy, the wayfarers and etc. Zakāt may be spent for food, shelter, education, health care, orphanages and other public services.

It is noteworthy that in many verses, paying zakāt is enjoined immediately after the command to perform one's prayers (*salāt*), and as a sign of faith and belief in God. Paying zakāt is an act of worship, so it must be performed for the sake of God. Therefore, not only does it help the needy and contribute to the establishment of social justice and development, but it also purifies the soul of those who pay it. The Qur'an says:

> Take alms from their wealth in order to purify and sanctify them (9:103).

Khums: Shi'a Muslims also believe in another obligatory tax, called *khums*. In Arabic Khums literally means one fifth. It is a 20% tax on the excess profit that a person annually makes. At the end of one's financial year, one pays 20% of all one's earnings after deducting house-hold and commercial expenses.[1] The obligation to pay khums has been mentioned in the Qur'an:

> And know that whatever profit you may attain, one fifth of it is assigned to God and the Messenger, and to the near relatives [of the Messenger] and the orphans, the destitute, and

---

[1] There are other cases mentioned in Shi'a jurisprudence in which paying khums becomes obligatory. What has been mentioned above is the most popular one.

the wayfarer, if you have believed in God and that which We sent down to our servant [Muhammad] (8:41).

Sunni Muslims usually believe that the verse only refers to what Muslims earn when they win a battle (booty) and consider it to be a type of zakāt.

According to Shi'i jurisprudence, half of the khums belongs to the twelfth Imam, the remaining member of the household of the Prophet and his successor, and the other half to the poor descendants of the Prophet, called "*sayyids*". Khums must be spent under the supervision of a Shi'a religious authority (*marji' al-taqlīd*), i.e. the grand jurist (*Ayatollah*) that one follows in practical issues. This is to make sure that it is spent in a way with which Imam Mahdi is pleased. The portion belonging to the Imam is usually spent on Islamic seminaries and other educational projects such as publishing useful books, or building Mosques, Islamic centres, and schools.

5. Struggle for the sake of God

Every Muslim has to struggle hard and strive for the sake of God in different ways to make improvements to human life in general and his individual life in particular. The Qur'an says:

He has created you upon the Earth and has asked you to develop it (11:61).

To be indifferent to human catastrophes or to be lazy in one's personal life is greatly condemned. On the contrary, the one who works hard to earn some money to spend on his family and improve their living conditions is considered as a hero in the struggle for the sake of God, a *mujāhid*. A very outstanding and vital case of this struggle (*jihād*) is to defend human rights such as liberty, freedom, and Islamic and human values such as justice, dignity, and a Muslim nation's integrity. The Qur'an says:

> Permission [to fight] is given to those against whom war is being wrongfully and offensively waged, and surely God is able to give them victory. Those who have been expelled from their homes unjustly, only because they said, "Our Lord is God…" (22:39-40).

> And why do you not fight for the sake of God and the utterly oppressed men, women, and children who are crying out, "O Lord! Rescue us from this town whose people are oppressors, and raise for us from You one who will protect, and raise for us from You one who will help" (4:75).

Of course, jihād also includes more personal cases in which one's family, property or reputation is endangered, usurped or damaged. According to Islamic traditions, one who is killed while defending his family or land achieves the same position as the soldier who is martyred in the warfront.

Jihād must continue until the just cause is achieved. The Qur'an says: "Fight against aggressors until oppression is stopped" (2:193). Of course, on a larger scale, a real jihād has always existed from the dawn of creation of mankind, between good and evil, truth and falsehood, and between the party of God and the party of Satan. This battle will more or less continue till the end of the time when the earth will be filled with justice under the government of al-Mahdi.

Jihād, whether it be with the pen, the tongue, a weapon, or any other means is an act of worship, and must be performed with pure intention, that is, only for the sake of

God and for just causes. No one is allowed to fight or struggle for materialistic purposes, for personal glory or the glory of any tribe, race, nation, or any other oppressive cause such as occupying others' land to become richer or more powerful. Indeed, jihād first of all starts within the inner self of a *mujāhid* (one who struggles). To make sure that one can win the external battle against evil, one has to fight first against his own lower desires and lusts, liberate his own heart from any satanic occupation, and regain the dignity and honour that God the Almighty has given human beings. The Qur'an says:

> O the soul at peace, return to your Lord, well-pleased (with Him), well-pleasing (Him). So enter among My true servants and enter into My Paradise! (89:27-30)

According to a well-known tradition, once, the Prophet Muhammad (peace be upon him and his family) said to a group of his companions who had won a battle: "Well-done! Welcome to those people who have completed the minor jihād (*al- jihād al-asghar*) and on whom the major jihād (*al-jihād al-akbar*) is still incumbent." Astonished, the companions who had defeated their enemies and were prepared to give up the dearest thing to them, i.e. their life to defend Islam asked, "What is the major jihād?" The Prophet Muhammad replied: "The major jihād is to fight against your own selves [or your souls]".[1] Thus, to resist one's temptations, and restrain one's soul from evil, and to purify one's self is the greatest and the most difficult jihād.

---

[1] *Al-Kafi*, Vol. 5, p. 12, no 3 and *Al-Amali* by al-Saduq, Session 71, p. 377, no 8. For an elaborate account of the subject, see *Combat with the Self* by Muhammad b. al-Hasan al-Hurr al-'Amili, translated by Nazmina Virjee (London: ICAS, 2003).

In conclusion let us refer to some of the merits of those who struggle for the sake of God as explained by God Himself:

> Those who believe, and have left their homes and strive hard with their wealth and their lives in God's way, are much higher in rank with God. These are they who are triumphant. Their Lord gives them good tidings of mercy from Him, and acceptance, and Gardens where enduring pleasures will be theirs. There they will abide forever. Surely with God there is a Mighty reward (9:20-22).

6. Enjoining good and forbidding evil

Enjoining good (*al-amr bi al-ma'rūf*) and forbidding evil (*al-nahy 'an al-munkar*) are two acts of worship that every mature Muslim has to perform whenever applicable. No Muslim can be indifferent to what happens in the world around him. Part of the social responsibilities of each individual Muslim is to observe human and religious values, and whenever any of these values is deliberately overlooked or violated, he must advise and direct those responsible towards performing good and against committing bad and sinful acts (3:103, 109 & 113; 7:199; 9:71 & 112; 22:41).

Chapter 4
ISLAMIC MORALITY

A proper way of studying Islam is to consider it as a *system*. Islam is not just a set of scattered beliefs and practices. Islam is not just a number of formalities which lack a unifying spirit. It is rather a complete system revealed by God to direct all aspects of human life throughout the ages and under different conditions.

Islam is a system, since it has all the mechanism required to meet the needs of mankind in its universality and entirety. Islam has clearly set up its ideals, and the theoretical and practical means to achieve them. The ability of Islam to cope with a very wide range of challenges and difficulties in all different ages, and to make steady progress under various cultural, social, economical and practical conditions without losing its identity and integrity, is a good sign of the high efficiency of the Islamic system of thought. Of course, Muslims admit that the main reason for this success and strength lies in Islam itself and not in the activities of Muslim rulers or the Muslim public.

I believe that there are three major characteristics of Islam: spirituality, rationality and the search for justice. Naturally, there are others that should also ideally be studied, such as dynamism, encouragement of the arts, sciences, and other aspects of civilization, and comprehensiveness. We have already talked about some aspects of rationality and justice.

In what follows, I will refer very briefly to aspects of Islamic morality as an entrance to Islamic spirituality.

Islam urges its followers to go beyond the material affairs of daily life and to seek out the real nature of human existence with its connections to the spiritual world. The process of cultivating spirituality can be summed up as follows:

1. attention to one's self (in contrast to negligence and immersion in material life);
2. knowing one's self, including its reality, faculties, potentialities and what benefits or harms it;
3. taking care of one's self.[1]

The process of taking care of one's self involves:

    a. acquiring appropriate beliefs and faith;

    b. refraining from evil deeds and performing acts of piety;

    c. acquiring good characteristics and removing evil ones;

    d. continuing the spiritual journey until one becomes a true servant who he meets his Lord.

---

[1] The Qur'an says:

> O you who believe! Take care of yourselves (or your souls); he who goes astray does not harm you when you are on the right path. (5:105)

Imam Ali says:

> Whenever the knowledge of a man increases, his attention to his soul also increases and he does his best to train and purify it. (*Mustadrak al-Wasā'il* by Nuri, Vol. 11, p. 323, no. 16)

"Meeting God" (*liqā'-u'llāh*) is a profound expression in Islamic mysticism. The expression has its root in the Qur'an. For example, the Qur'an says: "Anyone who is expecting to meet his Lord should perform good deeds and not associate anyone in the worship due to his Lord." (18:110) Of course, it is clear that it is not a physical meeting. Asking God for His guidance and provision for this journey, Imam Sajjad says:

> My God, so make us travel on the roads that arrive at Thee and set us in to motion on the paths nearest to reaching Thee!
>
> …. To Thee is the gladness of my eye, joining Thee the wish of my soul. Toward Thee is my yearning in love for Thee my passionate longing… Thy neighbourhood my request, nearness to Thee the utmost object of my asking…[1]

Based on the teachings of the Qur'an and the hadiths of the Prophet Muhammad and his household, Islam possesses an extremely rich heritage of spirituality built around the above elements. Whoever wishes to familiarize himself with Islamic spirituality must also know that it is a full-fledged system, penetrating all aspects of life. In Islam everything is devised in order to serve the spirituality of man and to facilitate his proximity to God, from religious practices such as praying and fasting to the social systems such as Islamic economics, politics and judicial laws.

Muslim mystics have studied different stations of the spiritual journey and explained the requirements of each

---

[1] The Whispered Prayer of the Devotee.

station. For example, Abu Abdullah al-Ansari (d. 481/1089) in his *Manāzil al-Sā'irin (Stations of the Wayfarer)* declares that he wrote this book for the benefit of a group of mendicants who were eager to know the various Stations or Milestones that the spiritual wayfarer must pass through in his journey towards God. He concisely studies one hundred stations. There have been many commentaries on this work as well as independent works on the same subject.

Unfortunately study of this journey falls outside the boundaries of this work. In the remaining part of this chapter we will just try to get acquaintance with aspects of the Islamic moral system along with a glance at the fruits and outcomes of living a life of faith and embarking on the spiritual journey.

Moral System of Islam

Moral teachings of Islam can be classified as follows:

I instructions about one's relationship with God;

II instructions about one's relationship with one's self;

III instructions about one's relationship with other people including one's family, relatives, friends, neighbours, strangers, clients, teachers, students, fellow-human beings, etc.;

IV instructions about one's relationship with the environment, including, animals, plants, air, water and other living and non-living beings.

There is a very rich literature pertaining to each category. In what follows, we try to refer to some examples from each category.

I Relationship with God

Remembrance of God: In many verses the Holy Qur'an commands the believers to remember God. For example, the Qur'an says:

> Remember your Lord much and glorify Him in the evening and the morning. (3:41)

> And remember the name of your Lord and devote yourself to Him with exclusive devotion. (73:8)

Remembrance of God has lots of advantages and benefits such as the serenity and tranquillity of the heart:

> Those who believe and whose hearts find serenity by the remembrance of God; now surely by God's remembrance hearts find serenity and tranquillity. (13:28)

The other benefit of remembrance of God is the luminosity of the hearts. In this regard, Imam Ali says:

> Certainly God, the Glorified, has made His remembrance the luminosity and shine of the hearts.[1]

Worship: God, in various verse of the Qur'an, commands us to worship Him sincerely and faithfully:

> Surely We have revealed to you the Book with the truth, therefore worship God being sincere to Him in obedience. (39:2)

Addressing Abraham, God says:

---

[1] *Nahj al-Balaghah*, Sermon 219.

> Say: surely my prayer and my sacrifice and my life and my death are all for God, the Lord of the worlds. (6:162)

Trust in God: There are many verses in which God commands the believers to trust Him:

> And on God should you rely and trust if you are believers. (5:23)

Repentance: In numerous verses God asks the believers to repent towards Him and ask His forgiveness:

> O you who believe! Repent towards God a sincere repentance. (66:8)

> And ask forgiveness of your Lord, then repent towards Him surely my Lord is Merciful, loving-kind. (11:90)

II Relationship with one's self

Purification of the soul: God puts emphasis on the purification and purity of human soul by swearing eleven times as follows:

> I swear by the sun and its brilliance, and the moon when it follows the sun, and the day when it makes manifest the sun (and her beauty), and the night when it covers the sun, and the heaven and Him who made it, and the earth and Him who extended it, and the soul and Him who made it perfect, then He inspired it to understand what is right and wrong for it. He will indeed be successful who purifies it and he will indeed fail whoever pollutes and corrupts it. (91:1-10)

Purification of the soul is a prerequisite for closeness to God. Indeed, the whole point in morality and spirituality is to purify one's soul. It is only then that the soul starts shining: receiving and reflecting outmost radiation and light from God. A major task of all the Prophets and an aim behind all their endeavours in teaching the divine message was to help people to purify their souls. The Qur'an says:

> He is the one who has sent amongst illiterate people an apostle from among themselves who recites to them His verses and purifies them and teaches them the Book and the wisdom. (62:2)

> Certainly God conferred a great favour upon the believers when He raised among them a Messenger from among themselves, reciting to them His communications and purifying them, and teaching them the Book and the wisdom, although before that they were surely in manifest error. (3:164)

Indeed, this was an answer to the prayer of Abraham and Ishmael after they raised the foundations of the House (*Ka'bah*):

> Our Lord! accept from us; surely You are the Hearing, the Knowing... Our Lord! and raise up in them a Messenger from among them who shall recite to them Thy communications and teach them the Book and the wisdom, and purify them; surely Thou art the Mighty, the Wise. (2:127-129)

These verses clearly show the great significance of the task of purification of the soul. The reason for such an emphasis is the fact that God is the most Pure and the most Perfect and it is only by the purification of the soul that we can have ambition of getting close to Him.

Self control: In this regard, the Qur'an says:

> And as for him who fears to stand in the presence of his Lord and forbids his own soul from its whims and caprices then surely the Paradise is the abode. (79:41 & 42)

> O David! …do not follow the whims of your own soul for they will lead you astray from God's path. (38:26)

> O you who believe…. Do not follow your low desires (the whim of your soul). (4:135)

In *Nahj al-Balaghah,* Imam Ali is quoted as saying:

> In the past I had a brother-in-faith, and he was prestigious in my view because the world was humble in his eyes… if two things confronted him he would see which was more akin to his whims and he would oppose it.[1]

Truthfulness: There is a great emphasis on truthfulness in the Holy Qur'an and traditions. I cite here some examples:

> O you who believe ! fear the wrath of God, and say only that which is true. (33:70)

> O you who believe! Fear the wrath of God and be with those who are truthful. (9:119)

After appointing Ma'adh b. Jabal as the governor of Yemen, the Holy Prophet told him:

---

[1] Wise-saying 281.

> I command you to fear God, tell the
> truth and keep your promises...[1]

Humbleness: In Islam arrogance is considered as a fatal deficiency of human soul and a major source for many sins and mistakes. According to the Qur'an, the reason that Satan refused to obey God and prostrate before Adam was his arrogance. On the other hand, humbleness is taken as a very great virtue. The Qur'an says:

> And the servants of the Beneficent God are those who go (walk) on the earth with humility and when the ignorant address them they reply peaceably and with great courtesy. (25:63)

> And do not treat people with arrogance, nor go about in the land exulting over much, surely God does not love any self-conceited boaster. (31:18)

Being moderate and balanced: As we said before, God has created the world with justice and asks human beings to observe justice. A requirement of justice is to give everything its due right and to strike a balance. Going to extremes leads to injustice to one's self or to others. In what follows, I will first mention one verse about the balance in general and then two verses about some specific cases in which the balance is required.

> And the heaven, He raised it high, and He made the balance, that you may not be inordinate in respect of the measure, and keep up the balance with equity and do not make the measure deficient. (55:7-9)

---

[1] *Bihar al-Anwar,* Vol. 74, p. 129.

They are the ones who, when spending of their sustenance for the sake of God, are neither extravagant nor miserly: as with everything else they practise moderation and strike a correct balance between the extremes. (25:97)

Neither speak your prayer aloud, nor speak it in a low tone, but seek a middle course between. (17:110)

Patience:

O you who believe! Seek assistance through patience and prayer, surely God is with the patient. (2:152)

O you who believe! Be patient and excel in patience and remain steadfast, and be careful of (your duty to) God, that you may be successful. (3:200)

Suppression of anger:

It (Paradise) has been prepared for those who suppress their anger. (3:137)

Avoidance of suspicion:

O, you who believe! Avoid most of suspicion, for surely suspicion in some cases is a sin. (49:12)

Imam Ali said:

Do not regard an expression uttered by any person as evil if you can find it capable of bearing some good.[1]

---

[1] *Bihar al-Anwar,* Vol. 71, p. 187.

Protection of tongue: The Prophet said:

> The salvation of the believer is in the protection of his tongue.[1]

> The belief of a person cannot be firm unless his heart is firm, and his heart cannot be firm unless his tongue is firm.[2]

Luqman said to his son:

> O my son! If you think that the speech is silver, surely the silence is gold.[3]

Pursuit of knowledge: Islam regards ignorance as a deficiency and the acquisition of knowledge as a virtue. The Qur'an says:

> One who has knowledge can never be equal to the one who is ignorant. (39:9)

The Prophet has said:

> It is the duty of every Muslim male and every Muslim female to seek knowledge.[4]

> Seek knowledge even if you have to travel as far as China.[5]

> If one leaves one's house with the intention of gaining knowledge, for every step that he takes,

---

[1] Ibid, Vol. 68, p. 286.

[2] Ibid, p. 287.

[3] Ibid, pp. 297 & 298.

[4] Ibid, Vol. 1, p. 177; Vol. 2, p. 32; Vol. 67, pp. 68 & 140; Vol. 105, p. 315.

[5] Ibid, Vol. 1, pp. 177 & 180.

God shall bestow upon him the reward reserved for a Prophet.[1]

Reasoning and reflection: The Qur'an asks people to use their reason (47 times), think (18 times) and reflect (4 times). For example, it says:

> In the creation of heavens and earth and in the difference between night and day are tokens for men of understanding. These are those who remember Allah, standing, sitting, and reclining, and consider the creation of the heavens and the earth, (and then cry out): Our Lord! Thou hast not created this in vain. Glory be to Thee! (3:190-191).

Imam Kazim says:

> Nothing more precious than reason has been given to people. The slumber of a man of reason is better than the worship of the ignorant throughout the night.[2]

Imam Askari says:

> Worship does not lie in engaging oneself in saying prayers endlessly or in fasting copiously, but in engaging oneself in the reflection on the divine affairs.[3]

Focus on one's own moral problems: Every Muslim needs to be an active member of society, be aware of what is going wrong in the society, and try to promote moral values.

---

[1] Ibid, p. 178.
[2] Ibid, p. 154.
[3] Ibid, Vol. 68, p. 325.

However, one should not forget his own problems and deficiencies. Imam Ali said:

> He who sees his own shortcomings (defects) keeps away from looking into other's shortcomings.[1]

Freedom from envy:

> Or do they envy the people for what God has given them of His grace? (4:54)

The Prophet said:

> Surely envy destroys the faith as fire destroys the firewood.[2]

III Relationship with other people

There are many instructions that govern relationships with others. Here we refer to some examples.

Fulfilling one's promise:

> And fulfil the promise surely (every) promise shall be questioned about. (17:34)

> And those who are faithful to their trusts and their covenant. (70:32)

Delivery of the trust:

> Surely God commands you to make over trusts to their owners. (4:58)

> If one of you trusts another then he who is trusted should deliver his trust. (2:283)

---

[1] *Nahj al-Balaghah,* Wise-saying 349.
[2] *Bihar al-Anwar,* Vol. 72, p. 252.

Pardon:

> And those who restrain (their) anger and pardon people. (3:135)

> They should pardon and turn away. Do you not love that God should forgive you? And God is Forgiving Merciful. (24:22)

The Holy Prophet said:

> May I lead you to the best moralities of this world and the life to come? These moralities are to regard him who disregard you, give him who deprived you (of his bestowals) and pardon him who wronged you.[1]

Imam Ali said:

> When you gain power over your adversary pardon him by way of thanks for being able to overpower him.[2]

Of course, if someone insists on his wrong actions or there is a systematic violation of others' rights the proper action is to speak to that person and ask him to stop his wrong actions. It is also recommended to cancel any debt that someone owes you and he is unable to repay.

Serving people: In Islam it is very important to render a service to fellow human beings. For example, the Qur'an reports that Jesus Christ said:

> And He has made me blessed wherever I may be. (19:31)

---

[1] Ibid, Vol. 68, p. 399.

[2] Ibid, p. 427.

Commenting on this verse, Imam Sadiq, the sixth Imam of the Shi'a, said:

> This means that God has made me very useful (for the people).[1]

The Holy Prophet said:

> To believe in God and to benefit His servants are the two highest characters.[2]

> God loves most the servants who benefit other servants most.[3]

> There are some servants (of God) to whom people resort in needs. They will be safe from the punishment on the Day of Resurrection.[4]

Safeguarding family: In addition to general instructions on how to treat other people, there are further instructions about certain groups of people. For example, due to its very high status in Islam there are many moral and legal guidelines for safeguarding and promoting family life. On philosophy of marriage, the Qur'an says:

> Among His sign is that He has created mates for you from among yourselves so that you find peace and tranquillity with them and He has established love and mercy between you. Surely there are signs in this for those who reflect. (30:21)

---

[1] Ibid, Vol. 14, p. 210.

[2] Ibid, Vol. 74, p. 139.

[3] Ibid, Vol. 74, p. 154; Vol. 93, p. 160.

[4] Ibid, Vol. 74, p. 159.

The Qur'an also urges members of the family i.e. husband and wife or children and parents to have love and mercy for each other. For example, we read:

> And treat them (women) kindly. (4:19)

On necessity of religious training of the members of the family, the Qur'an asks the believers to save themselves and their family members from going astray and doing wrong. (66:6)

According to Islam, family is a sacred institution and everything must be geared towards protection and promotion of family life. Divorce is permitted in Islam, but is considered to be the worst permitted act.

Respect for parents: Respect for, and obedience and kindness to, parents are enjoined upon Muslims. Unless the parents ask for injustice or sin to be committed, one needs to obey one's parents. The Qur'an says:

> And your Lord has commanded that you shall not worship none but Him and has commanded you to treat your parents with good will and respect. If one or both of them should live to old age, do not reproach them in the slightest or send them away in anger, but address them in terms of honour. (17:23 & 24)

> And He has enjoined on me to be dutiful to my mother. (19:31)

The Prophet has said:

> It is an act of worship to look at either parent with affection and kindness.[1]

---

[1] Ibid, Vol. 71, pp. 80 & 84.

> God is pleased when one has pleased his parents, and God gets angry when one has angered either parent.[1]

> Paradise lies under the feet of mothers.[2]

Hospitality: In Islam hospitality is considered as a very important virtue and indeed a test of belief in God and the Last Day according to the mass-transmitted (*mutawatir*) hadith of the Prophet Muhammad:

> Whoever believes in God and the Last Day, must treat his guest with respect and generosity.[3]

Guests are treated with courtesy and given what they need: sustenance, shelter and more importantly very warm welcome. The best treatment is to provide the guest with what the host has. Though the host is encouraged to give preference to his guest in using what is available, there is no need to go to great lengths, say, by borrowing money in order to buy new things or better food. The unexpected guests should not expect more than what is available. Those who fail to observe the obligation of hospitality should expect similar treatment when they meet their Lord in the Hereafter. On the other hand those who practice hospitality will be treated in an even better way when they arrive before the judgment of God, the eternal Host.

Respect for the elders: The Prophet Mohammad said:

---

[1] Ibid, Vol. 74, p. 151.

[2] Nuri, Mustadrak *Wasa'il al-Shi'ah*, Vol. 15. p. 180; Muttaqi Hindi, *Kanz al-'Ummal*, Vol. 16, p. 461.

[3] *Bihar al-Anwar*, Vol. 8, p. 144. This hadith has been also narrated by Al-Bukhari, Muslim, Malik, al-Tirmidhi, Abu Dawud, Ibn Majah, al-Darimi, and Ahmad.

> It is not one of us the one who does not show love and compassion to our kids or does not respect our elders.[1]

Visiting the sick: There are many traditions about the importance of visiting the sick and its etiquette, such as shortening the visit (unless the sick himself wishes to remain more), praying for the sick, talking to the sick about the blessings of God for the sick and taking some gifts to him. For example, we read in a hadith:

> The one who visits a sick will be encompassed by the mercy of God.[2]

Similar to what is mentioned in the New Testament (Matt. 25:31-46), we find in a tradition that on the Day of Judgement God will ask some people why they would not have visited Him when He was sick, why they would not have fed Him when He was hungry and why they would not have given water to Him when He was thirsty. Those people will ask: How could these have happened, while you are the Lord of the entire world? Then God will reply: So and so was sick and you did not visit him, so and so was hungry and you did not feed him and so and so was thirsty and you did not give water to him. Did not you know that if you had done so you would found Me with him?

Treatment of the sick: Life is one of the greatest gifts and blessings of God and, therefore, must be appreciated and protected. The guiding principle in Islamic medical ethics is mentioned in the Qur'an:

---

[1] *Bihar al-Anwar,* Vol. 72, p. 138.
[2] Ibid, Vol. 78, p. 215.

> If anyone has saved a life, it would be as if he has saved the life of the whole of mankind. (5: 32)

One way of saving lives of people is to treat them when they become sick. It is a mutual responsibility of the sick and the physicians (or society in general). In other words, seeking the treatment is a duty for the sick himself and everybody in the society is obliged to do the needful. On the necessity of treatment, the Prophet said:

> O servants of Allah, seek treatment, for Allah has not sent down any illness without sending down its treatment.[1]

This is a sample of a set of narrations that makes treatment mandatory when a treatment is available, and also if holding off this treatment would be harmful. On the other hand, healing people is considered as a sacred job. Indeed, the real healer is God Himself:

> And when I am sick, He restores me to health. (26: 80)

Respect for teachers and scholars: The Fourth Imam has said:

> Your teacher has the following rights. Firstly, total respect from you. Secondly that you listen attentively when he speaks. Thirdly, that you never raise your voice in his presence...[2]

---

[1] Ibid, Vol. 59, p. 76.
[2] Ibid, Vol. 2, p. 42.

Resisting oppression: As we saw earlier, Muslims are required to act with justice in all their dealings with others and in all circumstances. For example, the Qur'an says:

> O you who believe! Stand out firmly for justice, as witnesses to God, even though it be against yourselves, or your parents, or your kin, be he rich or poor... (4:135)

According to Islam, to suffer oppression passively is as bad as to commit oppression. He who makes no effort to alleviate the suffering of an oppressed one is an oppressor. In his advice to his sons, Imam Ali says:

> Be an enemy of oppressors and be a friend and helper of those who are oppressed.[1]

Charity: The Qur'an enjoins the spending of one's wealth in the way of God for the poor, the needy, the freeing of slaves, the curing of the sick and other good causes.[2] Charity is a precondition to the attainment of piety. For example, the Qur'an says:

> Those who spend their substance for the sake of God, and follow not up their gifts with reminders of their generosity or with injury,-for them their reward is with their Lord: on them shall be no fear, nor shall they grieve. Kind words and the covering of faults are better than charity followed by injury. God is free of all wants, and He is Most-Forbearing...And the likeness of those who spend their substance,

---

[1] *Nahj al-Balaghah,* Letter 47.

[2] For mandatory charity, please refer to the discussion about almsgiving in the Chapter Three.

> seeking to please God and to strengthen their souls, is as a garden, high and fertile: heavy rain falls on it but makes it yield a double increase of harvest, and if it receives not Heavy rain, light moisture suffices it. God sees well whatever you do. (2:262-265)

There are innumerable traditions of the Prophet and the Imams on the merits of charity. It has also been mentioned that "if you have nothing to give, offer at least a kind word or even just an affectionate smile."

IV Relationship with the environment

Both in His creation and legislation God has made human beings able to benefit from the nature. We read in the Qur'an:

> And He has subjected to you, as from Him, all that is in the heavens and on earth: Behold, in that are Signs indeed for those who reflect. (45:13)

> It is He Who hath created for you all things that are on earth... (2:29)

However, human beings must make use of the nature, and indeed every other gift and blessing, in a responsible way:

> Then on that day you shall most certainly be questioned about the blessings. (102:8)

Therefore, everything in the world which is at our disposal is both a gift and a trust. If it were just a trust we would not have permission to use them. Since they are gifts of God, we can use them. However, we cannot waste them or use them extravagantly as it is the case with any trust.

> And He it is Who produces gardens (of vine), trellised and untrellised, and palms and seed-produce of which the fruits are of various sorts, and olives and pomegranates, like and unlike; eat of its fruit when it bears fruit, and pay the due of it on the day of its reaping, and do not act extravagantly; surely He does not love the extravagant. (6:141)
>
> O Children of Adam! Wear your beautiful apparel at every time and place of prayer: eat and drink: But waste not by excess, for God does not love the extravagant. (7:31)

In addition to this, the Qur'an tells us that we are supposed to make efforts to improve the conditions of the globe as much as possible:

> He brought you forth from the earth and has asked you to improve it, therefore ask forgiveness of Him, then turn to Him; surely my Lord is Nigh, Answering. (11:61)

Therefore, we must be very careful about the way we treat the nature and environment. As an example, here I would like to refer to some of our moral and legal responsibilities in respect to animals. We find in Islamic hadiths that unjustified killing of animals or negligence towards their lives is very severely treated. For example, Imam Sadiq has informed about the divine punishment of a woman who had fastened a cat with the rope so that the cat could not move and died out of thirst.[1] A predominant scholar, 'Allamah

---

[1] *Bihar al-Anwar*, Vol. 76, p. 136.

Mohammad Taqi Ja'fari concludes his discussion about animals in this way:

> Consideration of whole sources of Islamic jurisprudence (*fiqh*) leads to the conclusion that animals must not be killed unless there is a legal permission (by God) like benefiting from them or being safe from their harm. There are adequate reasons for prohibiting hunting animals for fun and one can argue from them for prohibition of killing animals without having a permitting cause.[1]

The above idea is part of a broader Islamic perspective on animal life. According to Islam, there are many rights for animals that must be observed. Consideration of those rights show that not only their life must be protected, but also the quality of their life must be observed. For example, animals must not be bothered by forcing them to carry heavy goods or to move faster than they tolerate. Neither animals can be cursed or harassed. It is reported that Imam Ali said: "Whoever curses an animal he himself will be cursed by God."[2]

Outcomes of living a life of faith

Living a life of faith and observing moral values have great effects on one's life and bring about consequences on both the individual and the social planes, such as peace,

---

[1] *Rasa'il-e Fiqhi*, p. 250. Elsewhere he writes: "Hunting animals for amusement and without need is prohibited. Therefore, if someone makes a trip for such kind of hunting his trip is a sinful trip". (Ibid, p. 118)

[2] Ibid. cited from *Wasa'il al-Shi'ah*, Vol. 8, p. 356.

confidence, happiness and certainty as well as material blessings. Here we refer to some of those outcomes as described in the Qur'an and The Sunnah.[1]

Complete support by God: In a famous hadith, the Prophet reports that he asked God about the status of the believers, and God's answer included the following:

> None of My servants can seek proximity to Me by that which is dearer to Me than things that I have made obligatory to him. Then, with the performance of *nawafil* (the recommended acts), he continuously attains proximity to Me, so that I love him. When I love him, I will be the ear with which he hears, the eyes with which he sees, and the hand with which he strikes. If he calls Me, I will answer his call, and if he makes a request, I will grant it.[2]

Perfect knowledge: There are many hadiths which indicate that one of the consequences of having attained spiritual nearness to God is to be endowed with great knowledge of the realities of the world, including many mysteries that can never be known through ordinary methods of learning and teaching. Again the Prophet reports God as saying with regard to the servant who has attained proximity to Him:

> I will love him when he loves Me and I will make him loved by My creation, and I will open up his inward eyes to My glory and grandeur, and I will not hide from him [the knowledge of] the select of My creation. So in the darkness of

---

[1] For a discussion on some of the results of closeness to God, see *Self-Knowledge* by M A Shomali, 1996, pp. 148-158.

[2] *Usul al-Kafi*, Vol. 2, pp. 352 & 353.

night and in the light of day, I will tell him secrets, so that his conversations with creatures and with his companions will be cut off. I will make him hear My words and the words of My angels and I will reveal to him the secret I have hidden from My creation.[1]

Exclusive devotion to God: To be cut off from anything other than God means to be free from any reliance on anything other than God, and to see everything as His sign and as a manifestation of His power and grace. The true servants of God live within society while remaining totally mindful of God, and they remember Him continuously. The Qur'an praises a group of people "whom neither business nor trading distract from remembering God, keeping up prayer, and giving alms". (24:37) Imam Ali and other members of the household of the Prophet called upon God, saying:

> My God! Make me completely cut off from all else but You, and enlighten the vision of our hearts with the radiance of looking at You, until the vision of our hearts penetrates the veils of light and reaches the Source of Grandeur and set our spirit to be suspended at the glory of Your sanctity.[2]

Entrance to the realm of light: The above hadiths and many others refer to the fact that one of the consequences of progress on the spiritual journey is the elimination of

---

[1] *Bihar al-Anwar*, Vol. 77, p. 28 & 29.
[2] "Al-Munajat al-Sha'baniyyah" in *Mafatih al-Jinan*.

darkness and entrance into the realm of light. This fact is clearly expressed by the Qur'an.[1]

Immense love for God: The mystic is not the one who just loves God; rather he is the one who loves God alone, because his love or hatred for anything else is only for the sake of God. He wills and desires only what his Beloved wills and desires. He has no will or desire other than His. The mystic's love for God permeates his love for anything else.[2] Imam Sadiq says:

> The pure heart is the one that meets its Lord while it is free from anyone else.[3]

Nothing short of reaching God can satisfy the spiritual wayfarer. The Qur'an says:

> Surely! With the remembrance of God hearts come to rest. (13:28)

Imam Ali b. Husayn says:

> Nothing will cool my burning thirst, but reaching You; quench my ardour but meeting You, dampen my yearning but gazing upon Your face, settle me in my settling place without closeness to You.[4]

Witnessing God in everything: The real mystic is the one who witnesses God in everything. Imam Husayn says:

---

[1] For example, see the verses 2:257 and 5:16. The realm of light is an important topic in Islamic philosophy and mysticism.

[2] For a detailed account of love, see *Love in Christianity and Islam* (2005, 2nd edition) by M. Heydarpoor.

[3] *Al-Kafi,* Vol. 2, p. 16.

[4] *The Psalms of Islam*, pp. 251 & 252.

> O my God! Through the variety of Your signs (in the world of being) and the changes in states and conditions, I realised that the purpose is to make Yourself known to me in everything, so that I would not ignore You in anything.[1]

Imam Ali says:

> I saw nothing except that I saw God before it, with it and after it.[2]

It is obvious that the vision in question, for God, the Almighty, is infinitely exalted beyond the range of the physical eye. God cannot be seen by the physical eye, neither in this world nor in the hereafter.

The foregoing discussion demonstrates that Islamic spirituality is God-centred. The value of man, the subject of this journey and the best of God's creation, is defined by the place that he occupies on the path towards God, the most Perfect, by the degree that he is either distant from Him or close to Him.

Supplication

One of the manifestations of spirituality in Islam is supplication (*du'a*), a practice much emphasised in the Qur'an and the hadiths of the Prophet and his Household. For example, the Qur'an says:

> If My servant asks you about Me [tell them:] surely I am near. I answer the call of the caller when he calls Me. (2:186)

---

[1] "The Prayer of 'Arafah" in *Mafatih al-Jinan*.
[2] Sadr al-Din al-Shirazi, *Al-Asfar*, Vol. 1, p. 117, Vol. 4, p. 479 and Vol. 5, p. 27.

> Call Me! I will answer to You. (40:60)

The Prophet Muhammad said:

> Supplication is the weapon of the believer and the pillar of faith.[1]

There are many hadiths about different aspects of supplication, such as its meaning and purpose, instructions on how and when to make supplication, and the obstacles to supplications being answered. A very significant collection of supplications in Islam is *Al-Sahifat al-Sajjadiyyah* composed by Imam Ali b. Husayn.[2] This book is made up of 54 supplications, and is a masterpiece of Islamic spirituality that includes profound theological, philosophical and psychological facts as well.

---

[1] *Al-Kafi*, Vol. 2, p. 468.

[2] This book has been translated into English more than once. Perhaps the best translation is that made by William Chittick under the title *The Psalms of Islam*.

Chapter 5
THE MUSLIMS IN THE WORLD

Around twenty five percent of the world population (i.e. more than 1.5 billion) adhere to Islam. A breakdown of the Muslim population of the world in 2006 is estimated as follows:[1]

Continent	Population (million)	Muslim Population	Muslim Percentage
Africa	923.2	442.88	47.97
Asia	3.970.5	1.060.65	26.71
Europe	731.7	50.7	6.93
North America	331.7	7.13	2.15
South America	566.05	3.08	0.54
Oceania	33.54	0.6	1.79
Total	6.313.78	1.562.28	24.79

---

[1] For the sources of this statistics, see Muslim Population website at: www.islamicpopulation.com/world_general.html. However, according to some sources, the estimated percentage varies from 20 to 28.35 percent.

Muslims live all over the world. The total number of countries with Muslim inhabitants is 208.[1] About 85% of the Muslims live outside the Arab world.[2] The majority of Muslims live to the east of the borders of Iran, especially in Pakistan, India, Bangladesh, Malaysia and Indonesia. Indonesia is the most populous Muslim country.

Among Muslims, the Shi'a constitute at least about 10% of the Muslim population in the world.[3] According to some sources, the figure is 11%.[4][5] The Shi'a Islam is the majority faith in Iran, Iraq, Bahrain and Azerbaijan and has many adherents in Lebanon, India, Pakistan, Syria, Turkey and East Africa. The majority of Muslims are Sunni Muslims consisting of **Hanafis** (can be found in Egypt, Lebanon, Syria, Jordan, Iraq and Turkey), **Malikis** (dominant in Morocco and Sudan), **Shafi'is** (The Shafi'i school is applied in Syria, Yemen, Oman, the United Arab Emirates, Bahrain and Kuwait, and co-exists with other schools in Jordan and

---

[1] *Britannica, 2002,* Deluxe version. It adds: "Over the centuries the Shi'ite movement has deeply influenced all Sunnite Islam".

[2] For example see *Islam Outside the Arab World* (1999) by D. Westerland and I. Svanberg.

[3] For example, see *Britannica 2002,* Deluxe Edition.

[4] Yann Richard (1991, English translation 1995), p. 2 using mainly figures put forward by Md-R. Djalili, *Rligion et revolution*, Paris, Economica, 1981, p. 23ff, and M. Momen, *An Introduction to Shi'i Islam*, New Haven and London, Yale University Press, 1985, pp. 264ff.

5 Unfortunately, there are no accurate statistics reflecting the exact number of Muslims in general and Shi'a in particular. What suggested above is according to most of the sources available on the subject. However, it has been suggested that the Shi'a comprises 23% of Muslims, while the Hanafis comprise 31%; the Malikis comprise 25%; the Shafi'is comprise 16% and the Hanbalis comprise 4%. See S. M. Qazwini, p. 4, taken from the Bulletin of Affiliation: Al-Madhhab – Schools of Thought, vol. 17, no. 4 (December 1998), p. 5.

Egypt) and Hanbalis who hold the official school in Saudi Arabia and Qatar.[1]

Holy cities

Mecca

The holiest city in Islam, Mecca (in Arabic *Makkah*) is located in the Sirat Mountains in the western part of Arabia. The Sirat Mountains include Mount Hirā, which contains the cave where the Prophet Muhammad used to withdraw for reflection and worship before the beginning of his mission and where he also began receiving revelation. South of the city lies Mount Thawr (2,490 feet), which contains the cave in which the Prophet hid from the unbelievers during his migration to Medina. Within the city of Mecca lies the *Ka'bah*, the cube-like structure built by the Prophet Abraham and his son, Prophet Ishmael, on foundations originally built by the Prophet Adam. All Muslims orient themselves to the Ka'bah in their prayers.

Medina

The second holiest city in Islam, Medina (in Arabic *al-Madinah*), ancient Yathrib, is located in the western part of Arabia and is some 278 miles (447 km) distant from Mecca by road [215 miles (345 km) north of Mecca]. Unlike Mecca, Medina is situated in a fertile oasis. Before Islam, the city was inhabited mainly by two tribes, the Aws and the Khazraj, as well as Jews, some of whom anticipated the appearance of the last Prophet there.

---

[1] For example, see MEDEA (European Institute for Research on Mediterranean and Euro-Arab Cooperation), the entry for SUNNISM.

In 622 C.E., the Prophet Muhammad emigrated from Mecca to Medina. This emigration is adopted as the beginning of the Islamic calendar in both its lunar and solar forms.[1] Soon Medina became the capital of the Islamic state, founded by the Prophet Muhammad and continued to be so after the conquest of Mecca in 630.

Medina contains many important Islamic sites, including several mosques built in the time of the Prophet Muhammad and the tombs of great Muslim figures. The most important place in Medina, second only to Mecca in its holiness, is the Mosque of the Prophet (*Masjid al-Nabi*). Inside the Mosque are historically significant places such as the Prophet's pulpit (*minbar*) and the Prophet's place of prayer (*mihrab*). The small house of the Prophet Muhammad was situated next to the original mosque and was absorbed into it when it expanded. When the Prophet died, he was buried inside his house, and this has added to the religious and spiritual significance of the mosque in particular and the city of Medina in general. Every year, millions of Muslims, the Shi'a and the Sunni from all over the world, visit the mosque and the tomb of the Prophet Muhammad.

Other objects of pious visitation by all Muslims also include the Mosque of Qubā, where the Prophet said his prayers immediately after his arrival in Medina; the Mosque of the Two *Qiblah*s, where the Prophet was praying when the direction of the prayer was changed by God from Jerusalem to Mecca; and the tombs of Hamza, the uncle of the Prophet and other martyrs of the Battle of Uhud.

The graveyard of Jannat al-Baqi' is especially worthy of mention among other important sites in Medina. Many

---

[1] At the present time, it is the lunar year 1428 and the solar year 1386.

members of the family of the Prophet and his companions, as well as those who succeeded them, lie buried there. Jannat al- Baqi' is especially important for Shi'a Muslims, since it contains the tomb of Imam Hasan (grandson of the Prophet and son of Fatimah and Imam Ali and the second Imam of the Shi'a), Imam Ali b. al-Husayn (great-grandson of the Prophet, grandson of Fatimah and Imam Ali, and the fourth Imam of the Shi'a), Imam Muhammad b. Ali (the fifth Imam and son of the fourth Imam) and Imam Ja'far b. Muhammad (the sixth Imam and son of the fifth Imam). It is likely that Fatimah, daughter of the Prophet Muhammad, was also buried in Jannat al-Baqi', although she may have been buried inside the Mosque of the Prophet. The reason for this unique ambiguity is that according to her will she wanted her burial ceremony to be private and that her burial place to remain unknown to those who had vexed her in her lifetime.

Jerusalem

One of the holiest cities for all Muslims is Jerusalem (Bayt al-Maqdis, al-Bayt al-Muqaddas, or al-Quds). Among religiously significant sites inside Jerusalem is Masjid al-Aqsa ("the Farthermost Mosque"). Before the Ka'bah was established as the point of orientation for Muslim prayer, al-Aqsa was the place towards which Muslims were required to turn. This mosque is also the place from which the Prophet ascended to heaven on the night of the Mi'raj. The Qur'an says:

> Glory be to Him Who made His servant to go by night journey from the Sacred Mosque (*al-Masjid al-Haram*) to the farthermost mosque (*al-Masjid al-Aqsa*) of which We have blessed the precincts, so that We may show

to him some of Our signs; surely He is the Hearing, the Seeing. (17:1)

Najaf

The city of Najaf is located on a ridge (hence its name) in central Iraq, a few miles west of the Euphrates River and near the city of Kufa. The city was founded by the Caliph Harun al-Rashid in 791C.E. around the tomb of Imam Ali, the cousin and son- in-law of the Prophet, the fourth Caliph and the first Imam of Shi'a Muslims. The city has long been a centre of Shi'a pilgrimage and learning.

Karbala

The city of Karbala is located in central Iraq 55 miles (88 km) from Baghdad, on the border between the desert and the agricultural region. Karbala is one of the holiest places for the Shi'a Muslims, for this is where Imam Husayn and members of his family and his followers were buried after their martyrdom in the Battle of Karbala in 680 C.E. His shrine and that of his brother, Abu al-Fadl al-'Abbas, as well as the tombs of other martyrs are all located in Karbala. The old city containing the shrines is enclosed by a wall, and modern Karbala has grown to its south.

Kadhimayn

Kadhimayn is part of the city of Baghdad, the capital of Iraq. Originally the town was a cemetery belonging to the Quraysh, the tribe to which the Prophet and his household belonged. After their martyrdom, the seventh and ninth Imams of the Shi'a, Musa b. Ja'far al-Kazim and Mohammad b. Ali al-Jawad, were buried there. The place was frequently visited by those who loved the progeny of the Prophet, and gradually the town of Kadhimayn (in Arabic, the dual form of Kazim) was formed. In 336 A.H. Mu'izz al-Dawlah rebuilt the twin tombs. He also constructed a courtyard around the shrines lined with a series of rooms to house students of religion. There was also a lecture room on the eastern side of the shrine, called *"madrasa"* (place of study).

Samarra

The city of Samarra is situated on the east bank of the Tigris, seventy miles (97km) north of Baghdad. The city was founded between the third and the seventh centuries C.E. on the site of a prehistoric settlement dating to the 5th millennium B.C. In 836, the 'Abbasid caliph al-Mu'tasim made Samarra his new capital. The city kept growing till the Abbasid caliph al-Mu'tamid shifted the capital back to Baghdad. Samarra is regarded highly by Muslims, especially the Shi'a because the tenth and eleventh Imams, Ali b. Muhammad al-Hadi and al-Hasan b. Ali al-'Askari were confined there in a military camp by the Caliph of the time. Finally they were martyred and buried there. Before his occultation, the Twelfth Imam lived there too (255-260 A.H.). Unfortunately recently the terrorists attacked the shrine in Samarra twice and destroyed the dome in the first time and the minarets and the basement in the second time. These attempts were condemned by great majority of Muslims and non-Muslims from all over the world.

Mashhad

The city of Mashhad is situated in northeast Iran. Mashhad grew up around the site of the burial of Imam Ali b. Musa al-Rida, the eighth Imam of the Shi'a, who was martyred in 818 C.E.. Both the shrine and the city developed first under the Timurids in the 15th century and were greatly expanded by the Safavids from the sixteenth century onwards. Nadir

Shah (who ruled form 1736 to 1747) chose Mashhad to be his capital. Every year millions of Muslims, mainly the Shi'a, visit the shrine of Imam al-Rida. Mashhad is also the site of one of the leading Shi'a seminaries, from which many great scholars have graduated.

Qum

The city of Qum (or Ghom) is situated in north-central Iran, 92 miles (147 km) south of Tehran. Since the first century of Islam, Qum has always been one of the leading centres of knowledge and support for the school of the Ahlul Bayt. At the time of Hajjaj b. Yusuf al-Thaqafi, a group of the Shi'a from the Ash'ari clan migrated from Kufa to Qum and settled there. 'Abdullah b. Sa'd al-Ash'ari was their spiritual guide and teacher, and after him his children preached Islam and propagated the teachings of the Prophet and his household. Later, Ibrahim b. Hashim, a companion of the eighth Imam and a pupil of the great traditionist and scholar, Yunus b. 'Abd al-Rahman, settled in Qum and contributed to the cultivation of the Islamic sciences, especially the science of hadith.

In 816 C.E. Fatimah, sister of the eighth Imam, became ill while travelling from Medina to visit her brother in Marv, and she died in Qum. Her burial place in Qum has been visited by Shi'a Muslims generation after generation. In the 17th century a golden-domed edifice with tall minarets was built over the tomb. Several rulers and many scholars and saintly figures are buried in Qum

In 1340 (A.H.), Ayatullah 'Abd al-Karim al-Ha'iri, director of the Islamic Seminary of the city of Arak, went on pilgrimage to the city of Qum. Yielding to pressure from the scholars and people of the city, he decided to settle there and revive its institutions of learning. After victory of the Islamic

Revolution in Iran in 1979, led by Ayatollah Khomeini and his students and fellow scholars, Qum became the spiritual centre of the state, and greater attention was paid to the religious and academic institutions of Qum. Qum is now the leading centre of Islamic learning in the world. Hundreds of educational and research institutes and organisations operate there, and tens of thousands of students from Iran and other parts of the world are engaged in Islamic studies.

The important Mosque of Jamkaran is situated on the outskirts of Qum. According to historians, this mosque was built in Ramadan 393 A.H. by Hasan b. Muthleh Jamkarani in obedience to a command he had received from the Twelfth Imam. Every Tuesday and Thursday night, tens of thousands of pilgrims from different cities visit this mosque and perform their prayers there.

Bibliography

- Abd al-Jabbar (1384 A.H), *Al-Mughni fi al-Tawhid wa al-'Adl* (Cairo: Dar al-Kutub al-Misriyah)

- Ash'ari, Ali ibn Isma'il Abu al-Hasan, *Maqalat al-Islamiyin wa Ikhtilaf al-Musallin* (Beirut: Dar Ihya' al-Turath al-'Arabi)

- Askari, S.M. (1996), *Ma'alim al-Madrisatayn* (Tehran: al-Majma' al-'Ilmii al-Islami, 6th Imprint)

- Chittick, W. C. (ed. and trans.) (1981), *A Shi'ite Anthology* (Albany, New York: Sunny Press), Selected by S.M.H. Tabataba'i and Introduced by S.H. Nasr

- Fadli, 'Abd al-Hadi (1992), *Tarikh al-Tashri' al-Islami* (Beirut: Dar al-Nasr)

- Fakhry, M. (1991) *Ethical Theories in Islam,* Leiden: Tuta Sub Aegide Pallas

- Gilsenan, Michael (2000), *Recognizing Islam: Religion and Society in the Modern Middle East* (London & New York: I.B. Tauris & Co Ltd. Revised edition. First published in 1982 by Croon Helm. Reprinted in 1990 & 1993 by I.B. Tauris & Co Ltd).

- Haleem, M.A. (1997) "Early Kalam" in *History of Islamic Philosophy*, Vol. 1, edited by Sayyed Hussein Nasr and Oliver Leaman, (London: Routledge)

- Hilli, 'Allamah (1363 A.H), *Anwar al-Malakut fi Sharh al-Yaqut* (Qum: Radi and Bidar)

- Hilli, 'Allamah (1982), *Nahj al-Haqq wa Kashf al-Sidq* (Qum: Radi and Bidar)
- Ibn 'Asakir, *Tarikh Ibn 'Asakir, Tarjimah Ali* (Beirut: Dar al-Fikr)
- Ibn al-Athir (1421 A.H), *Al-Nihayah fi Gharib al-Hadith wa al-Athar* (Al-Dammam: Dar Ibn al-Jawzi)
- Ibn al-Athir, Muhammad (1415 A.H/1995), *Al-Kamil fi al-Tarikh* (Beirut: Dar al-Kutub al-'Ilmiyah)
- Ibn Hajar, Ahmad Haythami, *Al-Sawa'iq al-Muhriqah fi al-Radd 'ala Ahl al-Bid'ah* (Beirut)
- Ibn Hajar, al-'Asqalani, *Al-Isabah fi Tamyiz al-Sahabah* (Beirut)
- Ibn Kathir, Isma'il (412 A.H/1992), *Al-Bidayah wa al-Nihayah* (Beirut: Makatabah al-Ta'aruf)
- Ibn Khaldun, *An Introduction to History (al-Muqaddamah)*, English version, London, 1967 Edition.
- Iji, Abd al-Rahman b. Ahmad (1997), *Al-Mawaqif* (Beirut: Dar al-Jil)
- Ja'fariyan, R. (1985), *Ukdhubat Tahrif al-Qur'an bayn al-Shi'ah wa al-Sunnah* (Tehran: Islamic Propagation Organization)
- Kulayni, Muhammad (1397 A.H), *Usul al-Kafi* (Tehran: Dar al-Kutub al-Islamiyah)
- Lalani, Arzinia R. (2000), *Early Shi'i Thought: The Teachings of Imam Muhammad al-Baqir* (London: I.B. Tauris in association with The Institute of Ismaili Studies)
- Madelung, Wilfred (2001), *The Succession to Muhammad: A Study of the Early Caliphate* (Cambridge: Cambridge University Press. First published 1997 and reprinted 1997 & 2001).

- Majlisi, Muhammad B. (1983), *Bihar al-Anwar* (Beirut: Al-Wafa)
- Mufid, Shaykh Muhammad b. M. b. Nu'man (1413 A.H), *Awa'il al-Maqalat* (Qum: Kungereh-e Sheykh-e Mufid, 1413). In this edition the main text starts on page 33.
- Muzaffar, M.R. (1993), *The Faith of Shi'a Islam* (Qum: Ansariyan Publications).
- Nasr, S.H. (1989), *Expectations of the Millennium: Shi'ism in History* (New York: State University of New York Press)
- Nawbakhti, al-Hasan ibn Musa (1405 A.H), *Firaq al-Shi'ah* (Beirut)
- Pavlin, J. (1997) "Sunni Kalam and Theological Controversies" in *History of Islamic Philosophy Part 1*, edited by Seyyed Hussein Nasr and Oliver Leaman, London: Routledge
- Qazwini, Sayed Mustafa (2000), *Inquiries about Shi'a Islam* (California: The Islamic Educational Centre of Orange County)
- Richard, Yann (1991, English translation first published 1995), *Shi'ite Islam* (Oxford, UK & Cambridge, USA: Blackwell Publishers)
- Saduq, Muhammad b. Ali.b. Husayn b. Babawayh (1980), *Al-Amālī* (Beirut: Mu'assisat al-A'lam3)
- Saduq, Muhammad b. Ali.b. Husayn b. Babawayh, *Al-Tawhid* (Qum: Jamā'at al-Mudarrisin)
- Safi, Lutfullah, *Muntakhab al-Athar* (Tehran: Maktabah al-Sadr)
- Shahrestani, Muhammad ibn 'Abd al-Karim (1404 A.H), *Al-Milal wa al-Nihal* (Beirut: Dar al-Ma'rifah)

- Subhani, Ja'far (2001), *Doctrines of Shi'i Islam: A Compendium of Imami Beliefs and Practices* (London: I.B.Tauris), trans. Reza. Shah-Kazemi
- Subhani, Ja'far, *Al-Milal wa al-Nihal*, Vol. 6 (Qum: Imam Sadiq Inst.)
- Suyuti, Jalal al-Din 'Abd al-Rahman (1993), *Al-Durr al-Manthur* (Beirut: Dar al-Fikr)
- Tabari, Muhammad (1407 A.H), *Tarikh al-Umam wa al-Muluk* (Beirut: Dar al-Kutub al-'Ilmiyah)
- Tabataba'i, S. M. H. (1975), *Shi'ite Islam* (Albany, New York: Sunny Press), translated by Sayyid H. Nasr
- Tusi, Khajeh Nasir al-Din, *Talkhis al-Muhassal*, "The Treatise on al-'Ismah"
- Westerland, David & Svanberg, Ingvar (1999), *Islam Outside the Arab World* (Richmond: Curzon Press)

Note: References to hadiths from *Sahih* of Bukhari, *Sahih* of Muslim, *Sunan* of al-Nisa'i, *Sunan* of Abu Dawud, *Sunan* of Ibn Majah, *Sunan* of al-Tirmidhi, *Sunan* of al-Darimi and *Musnad* of Ahmad b. Hanbal are according to Sakhr serial number followed in *Mawsú'ah al-Hadith al-Sharif* (Version 1.1, 1991-1996).

Recommended reading list:

- ✓ *The Qur'an*, tr. 'Ali-quli Qara'i, London: Islamic College for Advanced Studies, 2005.
- ✓ Nasr, S. H. (2002), *Islam: Religion, History, and Civilization*, HarperCollins Canada.
- ✓ Nasr, S. H. (2004), *The Heart of Islam: Enduring Values for Humanity*, HarperCollins Canada.
- ✓ Schimmel, A. (1975), *Mystical Dimensions of Islam*, North Carolina University Press.
- ✓ Shomali, M A (2001), *Shi'i Islam: Origins, Faith & Practices*, London: Islamic College for Advanced Studies.